D1576306

VOLCANOES & EARTHQUAKES
GEOLOGIC VIOLENCE

McGRAW-HILL EARTH SCIENCE PAPERBACK SERIES

Richard Ojakangas, Consulting Editor

Bird and Goodman: PLATE TECTONICS

Cowen: HISTORY OF LIFE

Kesler: OUR FINITE MINERAL RESOURCES

Matsch: NORTH AMERICA AND THE GREAT ICE AGE

Oakeshott: VOLCANOES AND EARTHQUAKES: GEOLOGIC VIOLENCE

Ojakangas and Darby: THE EARTH AND ITS HISTORY

VOLCANOES & EARTHQUAKES
GEOLOGIC VIOLENCE

GORDON B. OAKESHOTT

Former Deputy Chief and Chief
California Division of Mines and Geology

McGRAW-HILL BOOK COMPANY

New York St. Louis San Francisco Auckland Düsseldorf Johannesburg
Kuala Lumpur London Mexico Montreal New Delhi Panama
Paris São Paulo Singapore Sydney Tokyo Toronto

This book was set in Helvetica by Black Dot, Inc. The editors were
Robert H. Summersgill and Carol First; the designer was
J. E. O'Connor; the production supervisor was Dennis J. Conroy.
Kingsport Press, Inc., was printer and binder.

VOLCANOES AND EARTHQUAKES: GEOLOGIC VIOLENCE

Library of Congress Cataloging in Publication Data

Oakeshott, Gordon B   date
    Volcanoes and earthquakes—geologic violence.

    (McGraw-Hill earth science paperback series)
    1. Volcanoes. 2. Earthquakes. I. Title.
QE521.02   551.2'1   74-31301
ISBN 0-07-047492-3

TO BETTY AND MARY

CONTENTS

SEVEN

EIGHT

NINE

TEN

ELEVEN

PREFACE

The most fundamental part of our environment is the earth on which we live and with which we have the closest contact. This is the realm of geology, the science of the earth. The materials of the solid earth—the rocks, their structure, their alteration by geologic processes, the fossil remains of ancient life in the rock formations—these are the tools the geologist uses to reconstruct the events of the history of the earth and its inhabitants throughout the vastness of geologic time.

Many geologic processes seem inordinately slow to us who live such a short span of geologic time. The uplift of a great mountain range, the carving of the Grand Canyon by running water, or the making of a Yosemite by water and ice are unbelievably slow as processes, however grand the product! Quite different are the activities and processes of volcanoes and earthquakes. Volcanoes and earthquakes are geologic violence. A crater-rim view of cascading and fountaining orange-red lava at Mauna Ulu on the East Rift of Kilauea in 1969, the 20-foot-high vertical scarp of a Hebgen Lake fault formed in the earthquake of 1959, the devastation wrought at Kodiak by the seismic seawaves which followed the great Alaskan earthquake of 1964, and riding through the intense ground shaking of the Long Beach earthquake of 1933, are among my unforgettable experiences of geologic violence.

It is something of the excitement of these experiences—and the excitement and stimulation of investigating the why and the how of such things— that I have tried to convey in this little book. There are no more beautiful and spectacular features of the landscape than great volcanic peaks like Mount Shasta and Mount Vesuvius, or grand fault scarps like the eastern face of the Sierra Nevada and the prominent rift-valley trench of the San Andreas fault in California.

I have not directed this book at my professional colleagues—although I hope they may enjoy browsing—but rather at those young people beginning the study of geology or geography in our secondary schools, community colleges, and universities, and at the many people who are interested in environmental and planning studies. Nowadays, we quite properly apply our knowledge of geologic processes and activities to the mitigation of geologic problems and to urban planning to avoid geologic hazards. Volcanic eruptions and earthquakes are examples of geologic violence, but they are not necessarily geologic hazards and need not be disasters. There is nothing basically "good" or "bad" in natural geologic events; there are no geologic hazards, or disasters, without people. We study the problems of volcanoes and earthquakes and we learn that there is much that intelligent and knowledgeable people can do to avoid disaster, or ease it when it threatens.

The text—replete with examples and organized around "case histories"—is arranged in four parts. Chapters 1 to 3 deal with an introduction to geologic time, geologic principles, volcanic processes, and the causes and features of volcanoes and earthquakes. Great natural disasters of history are discussed, and there is a chapter on moving crustal plates, their junctures, and their relationships to the causes of volcanism and faulting.

Chapters 4 to 8 discuss the making of volcanic rocks, Hawaiian and flood-basalt eruptions, Iceland on the mid-Atlantic ridge, hot springs and geysers, and volcanism through 4 billion years of geologic time.

Chapters 9 to 13 include observations on the great Owens Valley earthquake of 1872 and the features of faults; the San Andreas fault system, its earthquake history, and the elastic rebound theory; earthquake waves; and some great earthquakes of history.

Chapter 14 is about people, prediction, and protection. It considers the uses and benefits of earthquakes and volcanism, the problems and possible consequences of earthquake prediction, the monitoring of the activity of great volcanoes, and what people and governments can do about earthquakes.

ACKNOWLEDGMENTS

I am grateful to my principal editor, Richard W. Ojakangas, for constructive, overall criticism of the manuscript and for his thoughtful, painstaking attention to detail. The experience of readers Barry S. Haskell, Robert L. Heller, Lloyd J. Schmaltz, and Bruce A. Bolt in university and junior college teaching contributed to a more readable text.

Many of the beautiful photographs I owe to my colleagues of the California Division of Mines and Geology and of the U.S. Geological Survey. The unique scratchboard drawings and diagrams by my brother, Peter H.

Oakeshott, relieve the printed pages and add to clarity of the text. The typing was done by Margaret W. Turner, whose experience in typing geological manuscripts was a great help.

"Betty," in the dedication, is a long-time geological editor for the California Division of Mines and Geology, Elisabeth L. Egenhoff, who is now enjoying early retirement. "Mary" is Mary R. Hill who has nurtured and edited the Division's monthly, *California Geology*, and its predecessor, *Mineral Information Service*, for many years. The interested and dedicated help of these two highly competent people did much to establish the excellence of the state's technical publications, and both Betty and Mary have been inspiring to me during my 25 years with the State Division.

Gordon B. Oakeshott

VOLCANOES & EARTHQUAKES
GEOLOGIC VIOLENCE

ONE

GEOLOGIC TIME, GEOLOGIC PRINCIPLES, AND GEOLOGIC VIOLENCE

How old is the earth? Who is man, and how long has he been here? Or, has he always been here and has the earth always been here, much as it is today, unchanging, through the millenia? The oceans of the earth, the mountains, the plains, the volcanoes, the faults which cause earthquakes, and the rocks which underlie the surface features of the earth—how were they formed and what has been their history?

Study of the fossil remains of human beings—particularly the extraordinary finds during the last few years in east Africa—tells us that they probably evolved from earlier mammals sometime around 2 or 3 million years ago. This is but the last instant of geologic time, for geology—backed by astronomy—has shown that the earth is at least $4\frac{1}{2}$ billion years old. Rather late in the history of the earth, perhaps half a billion years ago, the more complex forms of life began to appear—evolving from simple, single-celled organisms in the seas of the earth.

The body of man was not greatly different from that of his predecessors, but the mind of man was distinctly larger and more complex than that of his forebears. Man's uniqueness lies in his capacity to think, particularly expressed in a profound curiosity about himself and his environment.

Clearly, the most fundamental part of our environment is the earth on which we live and with which we have such close contact. This is the realm of geology, the science of the earth. The materials of the solid earth—the rocks, their formation, and alteration by geologic process; fossils, the remains of life in the rock formations; and particularly reconstruction of the events of the history of the earth and its inhabitants throughout the vastness of geologic time—these are the concerns of geology. Thus, geology opens one of the principal doors through which we glimpse some of the answers to our curiosity about man's environment.

VASTNESS OF GEOLOGIC TIME AND THE PACE OF GEOLOGIC PROCESSES

Hundreds of years ago the old biblical scholars—like philosophers in the centuries B.C. and the scientists of today—sought a beginning, sought order out of chaos, and sought to explain the human race and its "dominion over every other living thing." And, of course, all through the most widely circulated of all books runs the central theme of search for the meaning of life and the uniquely human yearning for a future after death.

We recognize in the words of such scholars of old a certain concept of time, a recognition of change, or evolution, and an unexpressed sense of approach to events of the past through the things and natural happenings that made up the environment of people of those days.

Through the centuries since the beginnings of civilization—perhaps a hundred centuries ago when man first began to grow his own food and domesticate animals—man has increasingly applied the "scientific method" to his study of the earth and its inhabitants. Several centuries B.C., philosophers thought profoundly on these matters, basing their ideas on their beliefs and observations of nature and human beings, but with little of the scientific approach. Mathematics and astronomy were among the earliest scientific disciplines, followed in succeeding centuries by physics, chemistry, and the biological sciences.

What is the "scientific method," or the scientific approach to problems? Nothing very profound, complex, or mysterious! Essentially, it involves an investigative approach, systematically planned and carried out, with conclusions based on objectively obtained and objectively analyzed data. Scientific investigation and research originate with curiosity and are best pursued with imagination, disciplined by technical knowledge and competence. Through this sort of approach to a problem, a scientist may develop several "working hypotheses"—ideas for solutions—which may then be tested.

Geology blossomed as a science when the time was ripe, when civilization had developed the tools and attitudes of science. Particularly, geology grew as the basic principles of the sciences of chemistry, biology, and physics became operative.

As we look back on the history of the development of geology as a science, we find people and events of the early eighteenth century that mark great advances in understanding of the solid earth. Foremost among them is that shining star, James Hutton (1726–1797), who has been deservedly dubbed the "father of geology." A resident of Edinburgh and a physician, he roamed Scotland and England making field observations. Hutton had most of the requisites for success as a scientist and geologist: (1) his training as a physician which gave him a good background in science of his day, (2) curiosity about the earth's features he saw which helped him to recognize critical questions and problems, (3) an observational investigative approach, (4) the intelligence to systematically analyze and interpret his data, and (5) the depth of understanding to draw some profound conclusions.

I said he had *most* of the requisites for success. Alas, he was a poor and dull writer! Fortunately for the youthful science of geology, Hutton's friend, John Playfair, a professor of mathematics and philosophy, was a good and lucid writer and gave the young science of geology Hutton's great principles in *Illustrations of the Huttonian theory of the earth*, published in 1802, after Hutton's death. Few of us have the bold, new ideas of a Hutton, but how many of us greatly need a Playfair to competently and unselfishly frame and record our thoughts, pleasingly and effectively for posterity!

Hutton's keen observations of natural processes and natural forces operating on the earth of his day led him to formulate the fundamental geologic principle that the same processes and the same forces must have operated in much the same ways in the past. Quoting Playfair: "Amid all the revolutions of the globe the economy of Nature has been uniform, and her laws are the only things that have resisted the general movement. The rivers and the rocks, the seas and the continents, have been changed in all their parts; but the laws which direct those changes, and the rules to which they are subject, have remained invariably the same." For instance, rocks have always weathered to form soils, rivers have eroded the hills and reduced their levels, sediments have always been deposited in layers in bodies of water. Intermittently, throughout the history of the earth there have been active volcanoes erupting much the same products and in much the same ways as they do today; faults have broken the crust of the earth from time to time and earthquakes have accompanied such breaks, whether people were here to feel the shaking or not. What we are saying is that the "key to the past lies in the present." This thought, sometimes called the principle of *uniformitarianism*, is the basis for our interpretations of the record of past history in the rocks of the earth.

Hutton knew that geologic time must be immensely long if canyons were to be carved by the erosive action of running water and if mountains could be elevated to thousands of feet in height by upward movements so extremely slow as to be imperceptible in the lifetime of a man. We have much better quantitative measures of these things today. We know that about 2 million years has been eough time to erode the Grand Canyon to a depth of 5,000 feet in the high Colorado Plateau. A thin, black flow of lava spilled over the rim of the Grand Canyon and stopped on the floor of the canyon when it had been eroded to within 50 feet of its present depth. This flow has been radiometrically dated at 1.8 million years. It has been calculated that about 9 vertical miles of rock was removed from the crest of the Sierra Nevada in some 25 million years—roughly a lowering of the Sierran crest an average of 1 foot per 5,000 years. When we realize that great canyons have been carved from rock countless times in the past, and that mountain ranges have been built, eroded to low elevations and built again, and that layers of sediments have accumulated in some basins on the earth to a thickness of 50,000 feet, we gain some concept of the immensity of geologic time! Given enough time, great changes may, indeed, take place. *Change* has been a keynote of earth history. Nothing has remained static; the earth and geologic processes are dynamic—ever changing, ever moving, and constantly evolving through time.

How old is the earth? We return to our opening question. Scientists are much better equipped today to give quantitative answers to this query than in Hutton's day. Even by the end of the nineteenth century we knew little beyond the probability of an earth history of many millions of years. Time calculated for the earth to cool, for the oceans to reach their present saltiness, and for over 10 miles of sediment to accumulate to form layered rock was measured in terms of 40 to 100 million years.

Then, in the 1890s, came a great breakthrough in knowledge which advanced science a giant step above the levels of earlier knowledge: It was discovered that radium, thorium, uranium, and many other elements spontaneously emit radiation by the breakdown of their atomic nuclei—a property called *radioactivity. This gave the world a new concept of the sources of heat and energy in the earth. One of the important by-products of the discovery of radioactivity was the development of radiometric dating*—the use of radioactivity to determine the ages of rocks in years. Rates of decay for the isotopes of the radioactive elements that occur in rock minerals are constant, not affected by chemical or physical changes. Thus, we have a tool that enables us to calculate the number of years since the minerals cyrstallized. Igneous rocks—all of which have solidified from molten material in the earth—are ideally suited to dating by radiometric means. Time zero for the radiometric clock is the moment a mineral bearing a radioactive element crystallizes. Igneous rocks include *volcanic* rocks, which have formed from molten *lava* at, or near, the surface of the earth, and *plutonic* rocks which have formed from molten *magma* at depth.

Having once been molten, the earth itself is a gigantic mass of igneous rock. By searching out the oldest rocks on the earth and dating them radiometrically we can arrive at a minimum age of the earth in years. Over the last three-quarters of a century the tools, the methods, and the data for radiometric dating have been developed and improved to the point that we have reasonably precise figures for the age of the earth and for the divisions of geologic time (Table 1-1). Modernizing our methods and expanding our data have constantly lengthened concepts of the age of the earth! In the 1920s, geology textbooks estimated the age of the earth at about 1 billion years. This had been extended to about 2 billion by the early 1940s, and today the age of the earth (also the moon and meteorites) is measured radiometrically at $4\frac{1}{2}$ billion years. Thus, we seem to be reinforcing Hutton's theory of the earth expressed nearly 200 years ago, including his statement that "in the economy of the world, I can find no traces of a beginning, no prospect of an end."

Astronomy, using totally different approaches to the ages of the universe and its constituent bodies, generally confirms the latter figure for the age of the solids in our solar system. But astronomy goes farther to say that our sun probably originated some 6 billion years ago and still has about 6 billion

Table 1-1 Geologic time scale

ERAS	PERIODS, EPOCHS	TIME, MILLION YEARS	SOME GREAT EVENTS IN EARTH HISTORY
Cenozoic	Quaternary Recent or Holocene	0.01	All of the present world's great volcanoes on the lands originated during this time
	Pleistocene	3	
	Tertiary Pliocene	11	Mountain building, faulting, and intermittent volcanism very widespread
	Miocene	25	
	Oligocene	40	
	Eocene	60	Building of the Rocky Mountain System
	Paleocene	70	
Mesozoic	Cretaceous	135	Flood basalts in Brazil and in the Deccan Plateau of India
	Jurassic	180	Sierra Nevada, Coast Ranges of California, Cascade Range, and others built
	Triassic	225	Fissure eruptions in eastern North America
Paleozoic	Permian	270	Extensive and increasing mountain building and volcanism in parts of most continents
	Pennsylvanian	305	
	Mississippian	350	
	Devonian	400	
	Silurian	440	
	Ordovician	500	
	Cambrian	600	Volcanic activity in Europe
Precambrian	Late	1,800	Great thicknesses of volcanic rocks in the "shield" areas of the continents; plateau basalts
	Early	2,700	Oldest rocks and mountains
Crust of the earth solidified about 4,000 million years ago		4,500	Origin of the earth Continuous worldwide volcanism

years of life ahead of it. There is evidence to support the concept that the universe began with an explosive "big bang" more than 10 billion years ago and has been expanding at an enormous rate ever since. Even further, the universe may be a pulsating—or "breathing"—mass undergoing an enor-

Figure 1-1 View east up Yosemite Valley; El Capitan on left, and Half Dome in middle distance with Tenaya Canyon to its left. Bridal Veil Fall, on right, emerges from a hanging valley. Sentinel Rock is the ragged rock mass to right of Half Dome. John Muir, camped at the base of Sentinel Rock, was awakened at 2:30 on the morning of March 26, 1872, by tremendous rockfalls caused by the Owens Valley earthquake. The sheer face of El Capitan is about 3,000 feet high. (*Mary R. Hill photo.*)

mously long series of expansions and contractions each lasting about 100 billion years. In this sort of thinking, man is getting beyond his capacity; we simply cannot visualize a universe of infinite size, with no beginning and no end!

CATASTROPHIC ACTION OF VOLCANOES AND EARTHQUAKES
Many geologic processes and events seem inordinately slow to us whose lives are so short in terms of geologic time. We seldom see much change in the rock formations and landforms that make up the solid-earth part of our environment—except for what man does himself with bulldozers and graders!

Scientists—including geologists—in the nineteenth century were slow to accept the principles of uniformitarianism and the great length of geologic time proposed by Hutton and Playfair. Even they could have had no real appreciation of the vastness of geologic time, because they lacked the tools and the data we now have. Acceptance of these great ideas so essential to reconstructing the geologic history of the earth and earth's features came slowly. Many geologists of the nineteenth century preferred to explain the especially striking features of the landscape as due to abrupt and violent "cataclysms of nature."

J. D. Whitney, State Geologist of California in the 1860s, later explained the great gash of Yosemite Valley (Figure 1-1) on the western slope of the Sierra Nevada in California as due to cataclysmic rending apart of the granite rock as the mountains of the Sierra were violently uplifted. Naturalist John Muir, based on intimate knowledge of the Sierra, and particularly the Yosemite, bitterly disagreed with Whitney. Muir ascribed the flat-floored Valley, bounded by near-vertical walls over 3,000 feet high, to erosion by glaciers. We now know that for many millions of years—from about 40 to 60 million years ago to about 10 million years past—the Sierra Nevada remained a range of rolling hills with peaks like Mount Whitney perhaps 4,000 feet above sea level. Yosemite was then one of many western-Sierra valleys being slowly downcut by river erosion. Then, about 10 million years ago uplift and westward tilting began, continuing spasmodically to the present day. The uplift and westward tilting greatly increased the velocities of streams running down the western slopes and so they deeply cut into the rocks to form deep narrow valleys with V-shaped cross profiles. Such a valley was Yosemite, when a cooling climate with higher snowfall began to develop glaciers in the Sierran valleys about 3 million years ago. Stream erosion changed to glacial erosion as moving ice broadened the valleys and undercut their sides. For the last 30 million years, almost continuous volcanism in various parts of the Sierra has furnished a radioactive time clock which has enabled geologists to reconstruct the sequence of events in the building of the Sierra Nevada. Thus, a true understanding of geologic principles delineated 175 years ago, plus modern techniques of dating volcanic rocks, has enabled geologists to restore and date significant events in the building of this great mountain range.

We should not imagine that such processes as weathering, erosion, sedimentation, and uplift are always slow and unspectacular. Each, in certain circumstances, may be awe inspiring in the grandness of its force and action. In 1964, flooding rivers in northern California with their increased power of erosion uprooted giant redwoods hundreds of years old. In 1973 the Mississippi River in flood stage spread out over a hundred miles wide across the nearly flat Mississippi Valley. Even in normal times the Mississippi dumps almost 400 million tons of sediment into the Gulf of Mexico in a year.

Nevertheless, for sheer grandeur of catastrophic geologic action, nothing surpasses great volcanic eruptions and earthquakes! In spite of our age of scientific knowledge and sophistication, earthquakes and volcanoes can strike terror in the hearts of men. Both are frequent and current events in the history of mankind, and geology opens our eyes to the evidences of volcanic and earthquake history in every geologic age since the world was born. Let us look at a great earthquake and a great volcanic eruption, to illustrate geologic violence.

Alaskan Earthquake Late on the afternoon of Good Friday, March 27, 1964, one of the strongest earthquakes ever recorded shattered coastal Alaska

(Figure 1-2). This was nothing new for the Alaskan coast, for at least six truly great earthquakes have occurred in coastal Alaska from Yakutat to the Aleutians since 1899. Total energy of the Good Friday earthquake was greater than that of the San Francisco earthquake of 1906. Strong shaking in Alaska lasted about 4 minutes, an extraordinarily long time when we consider that the San Francisco earthquake had a duration of about 40 seconds.

The point on the surface where the shock appeared to have originated (the *epicenter*) was in an uninhabited area of glaciers, fiords, and the rugged Chugach Mountains about 75 miles east of the city of Anchorage and an equal distance northwest of Cordova. The earthquake was caused by movement along a fault, or break in the earth, at a depth of about 60 kilometers (40 miles). This point of apparent origin, vertically beneath the epicenter, is called the *focus* of the earthquake. Most earthquakes, as we shall see later, are caused by movement along faults.

In a 2-month period there were about 12,000 aftershocks strong enough to be felt by someone favorably placed. Of Alaska's sparse population, 114 people were killed and property damage was about $350 million.

In Alaska, as much as 80,000 square miles of land was uplifted or down-dropped by several feet in an instant. Former shelf areas below sea

Figure 1-2 Collapse of external walls and near-destruction of J. C. Penney Building, Anchorage, in the great Alaskan earthquake of 1964. The five-inch-thick reinforced concrete facing had fallen off and been removed at the time this picture was taken. (*From the photo file of the California Division of Mines and Geology.*)

level became dry land; on the large Montague Island, maximum uplift along faults, or breaks in the ground, was 33 feet! Land surfaces in other areas subsided below sea level. Docks at Cordova were elevated about 11 feet above their normal position in relation to sea level. Deformation of the earth's surface was the most extensive ever related to an earthquake. A northeast-trending uplifted strip of the earth's crust over 100 miles wide and 500 miles long extended southwest of Cordova and Valdez; farther northwest, a down-dropped strip of similar dimensions extended southwest of Anchorage through Homer and Kodiak Island.

Secondary effects of the earthquake included hundreds of landslides, rockslides, avalanches, and cracks due to shaking and lurching. The city of Anchorage, population about 50,000, lies on a silty plain which accumulated as a result of melting glaciers and which slopes from the base of the Chugach Mountains down to the sea, where it drops off abruptly along a series of bluffs about 30 to 50 feet above sea level. When the tremendous shaking of the earthquake occurred, the layers of clay and silt underlying the plain failed and broke into 200 acres of slides that carried some of the fine homes of Turnagain Bluff out toward the sea as much as 500 feet. In downtown Anchorage, blocks of earth along L Street, Fourth Avenue and Government Hill dropped several feet, breaking up buildings and carrying them with the earth. In some places sliding extended below sea level as well as above; for example, the docks at Valdez, along with 30 people who were waiting for a merchant ship to come in, were carried out to sea by sliding of glacial sediments in a subsea delta. Plant and animal life all along the coasts near sea level, above and below, were profoundly affected by the changes in relative level of land and sea.

Seismic sea waves (*tsunamis* or "tidal waves") generated by abrupt ocean-floor movements and by submarine landslides traveled to points all around the north Pacific, damaging coastal towns such as Homer and Valdez in Alaska and Crescent City, California. At Crescent City, 12 people were killed when the sea wave, still 20 feet high, hit the coast. Inland bodies of water as far away as Florida were affected by *seiches*, the rhythmic sloshing of water due to earthquake ground waves.

Eruption of the Volcano Krakatoa Since we are speaking of superlatives in geologic violence, we might mention one of the greatest volcanic eruptions of all time: that of Krakatoa, a small island between Java and Sumatra in the East Indies, in 1883. The region was known to be of volcanic origin; ages ago a huge eruption had left a circular group of islands when a great volcano blew its top. One of these islands was 2,623-foot-high Krakatoa, which had been inactive for over 200 years. Premonitory signs of the major eruption were minor explosive discharges of dust and *pumice* (mostly fine fragments of volcanic glass) beginning about 6 years before. Then on August 26, 1883, began a 3-day series of some of the most violent explosions ever seen and heard by man. A cubic mile of fragmented rock was thrown into the air as high as 17 miles, followed and accompanied by explosions of volcanic dust and *ash* (small fragments of volcanic material). The hole left in the ocean was 1,000 feet deep.

Sounds of the explosions were heard 5,000 kilometers away and the earth was shaken by strong local earthquakes within a radius of 100 kilometers. Dust entered the upper atmosphere and traveled around the earth for months before most of it settled. I can remember my father telling me that, as a fifteen-year-old boy in London, he was fascinated by fantastically colored sunsets—green, for instance—beginning a few weeks after the eruptions of Krakatoa. The eruptions so disturbed the sea floor in the volcanic region that huge seismic sea waves were set up. These inundated the low coasts of Java and Sumatra, destroying whole towns and killing at least 36,000 people, many times the number killed directly by the volcanic eruption.

SUMMARY
The concerns of the science of geology are the materials of the solid earth on which we live—the rocks, and their formation and alteration by geologic processes; fossils, the remains of life in the rock formations; and particularly, the reconstruction of the events of the history of the earth and its inhabitants through the vastness of geologic time.

Geologic time is enormous—$4\frac{1}{2}$ billion years since the earth was born—and geologic processes are usually slow in terms of the short span of life of a human being. While geologic processes—like weathering, erosion by running water, volcanism, and faulting—have not changed through time, *change* has been a keynote of earth history. No landscape has remained unchanged through time. Fundamental to the study of the geologic sciences are concepts of (1) the vastness of geologic time, (2) a constantly changing earth through geologic processes, and (3) geologic processes which have followed the same physical laws and have acted in the same way through time.

Volcanism and earthquake activity are complex geologic processes which involve all physical processes, but volcanoes and earthquakes may be spectacular and intermittently violent in their action. For sheer grandeur of catastrophic geologic action, nothing surpasses great volcanic eruptions and earthquakes!

The study of geology—like learning in other sciences—should be approached through investigations, systematically planned and carried out. Geologic observation, investigation, and research originate with curiosity and are best pursued with imagination, disciplined by technical knowledge and competence.

How do we start?

In this little book we are dealing with the spectacular; we have started with geologic violence. But should you pursue these studies to become a volcanologist or a seismologist, you would find that you would have to learn about all sorts and types of geologic processes and activities, ranging from sea-floor spreading to erosion and deposition by running water and moving ice.

TWO

GREAT NATURAL DISASTERS

EARTH HAZARDS TO HUMAN LIFE AND PROPERTY—IN PERSPECTIVE
What is the value of a human life, in dollars?

We can readily appraise the value of a section of land or any other piece of property. But how much value does society place on my life? Or yours? Impractical, if not impossible to compute! Nevertheless, society makes such decisions daily, all over the world.

Hazard implies a possible exposure to danger; *earth hazard* or *geologic hazard* suggests that the danger is due to a natural cause—what the law has often called an "act of God," implying that it is beyond our control. *Risk* implies taking a chance on death, injury, or loss of property. How much chance are we willing to take; that is, what is "acceptable risk"?

Natural earth processes may all be hazards at certain times and under certain circumstances, but most are not sudden disasters without warning because most are predictable, or at least expectable, and we can do something about most of them. Where there are people, normal earth processes and features may become hazards. Earthquakes, volcanoes (Figure 2-1), floods, landslides, storms, mud flows, erosion, deposition, seismic sea waves, land subsidence, wave action, avalanches, glaciers, all may be hazards. But it lies within human knowledge and human resources to successfully live with all of them. Geology teaches us something of the nature of the problem—*what* to expect, more or less *when* to expect it, and a great deal about *what to do* about it!

Figure 2-1 Lassen Peak, California, in eruption in August 1915. (*Drawn by Peter H. Oakeshott from an old photo.*)

Mary R. Hill of the California Division of Mines and Geology has tabulated for us some of the world's worst historic disasters (Tables 2-1 and 2-2). Wars are not even included in the table, but wars—entirely man-made—have accounted for the loss of untold millions of lives. Also not included are automobile traffic deaths, the largest of all causes of deaths from hazards in the United States. But these are too common; have we accepted high traffic risk? Man's knowledge has greatly reduced losses from disease; bubonic plague, for instance, is a thing of the past, and flu is gradually coming under control. Natural disasters—floods, weather, landslides, and earthquakes—have cost most lives in the world's areas of large population density and least education.

Our special interests—earthquakes and volcanoes—have not been responsible for most of the world's greatest disasters, but still they rank far too high as causes of violent death.

EARTHQUAKE RISK

Earthquakes fall in that category of *expectable* geologic hazards, but not yet *predictable* in terms of precise time, place, and energy. What are the possibilities of damaging shocks within a given time at a given place?

Table 2-1   Some historic disasters

YEAR	DISASTER	DEATHS
1347–1351	Bubonic plague, Europe and Asia	75,000,000
1556	Earthquake, China	830,000
1871	Forest fire, Wisconsin	1,000
1878	Famine, China	9,500,000
1881	Typhoon, Indochina	300,000
1883	Eruption of Krakatoa, East Indies	36,000
1887	Flood, China	900,000
1902	Eruption of Mont Pelée, West Indies	40,000
1912	Sinking of the Titanic	1,500
1918	Influenza, worldwide	22,000,000
1920	Landslides, Kansu, China	200,000
1925	Tornado, south central United States	700
1928	Collapse of St. Francis Dam, southern California	500
1933	Long Beach, Calif., earthquake	115
1941	Snow avalanche, Peru	5,000
1942	Mine explosion, Manchuria	1,500
1944	Train wreck, Italy	500
1956	Sinking of the Andrea Doria	1,600
1960	Airline collision, New York	134
1963	Rockslide into Vaiont Reservoir, Italy	2,000
1964	Alaskan earthquake	114
1971	San Fernando, Calif., earthquake	64

Judging the potential for earthquake damage in any given area is fraught with difficulties. There are too many factors which are imperfectly known or understood. However, given a moderate-to-great earthquake, the most important factors affecting damage to property and loss of life are the density of population and type of building construction. Obviously, it is our great metropolitan centers that are vulnerable, and the poorly built works of man in such areas will be the centers of death, injury, and property loss (Table 2-2). Any major earthquake is felt over an area of 100,000 square miles or more, so the effects of a big earthquake are not only local.

Let us look first at what happens in a moderate-to-great earthquake to get a better idea of the sort of risk involved.

THE EARTHQUAKE—GROUND SHAKING   First to be considered is the earthquake itself, that is, the ground motion. In a moderate-to-strong earthquake this is intense enough within a few miles of the epicenter to make it difficult for an adult to keep his feet. In the moderate 1933 Long Beach, California, earthquake I was unable to stand, except by hanging onto a doorframe. Such strong motion may last from a few seconds in a moderate earthquake to as much as 4 minutes (Alaska, 1964) in a great earthquake. There is often exaggerated ground motion on loose, water-saturated ground; ground movement is much less on solid rock. In great earthquakes, a long, strong,

Table 2-2 Some of the most disastrous earthquakes

YEAR	PLACE	DEATHS
856	Corinth, Greece	45,000
1038	Shansi, China	23,000
1057	Chihli, China	25,000
1170	Sicily	15,000
1268	Silicia, Asia Minor	60,000
1290	Chihli, China	100,000
1293	Kamakura, Japan	30,000
1456	Naples, Italy	60,000
1531	Lisbon, Portugal	30,000
1556	Shenshi, China	830,000
1667	Shemaka, Caucasia	80,000
1693	Catania, Italy	60,000
1693	Naples, Italy	93,000
1731	Peking, China	100,000
1737	Calcutta, India	300,000
1755	Northern Persia	40,000
1755	Lisbon, Portugal	30,000–60,000
1783	Calabria, Italy	50,000
1797	Quito, Ecuador	41,000
1811–1812	New Madrid, Mo., U.S.A.	0(?)
1819	Cutch, India	1,500
1822	Aleppo, Asia Minor	22,000
1828	Echigo (Honshu), Japan	30,000
1847	Zenkoji, Japan	34,000
1868	Peru and Ecuador	25,000
1875	Venezuela and Colombia	16,000
1896	Sanriku, Japan	27,000
1897	Assam, India	1,500
1898	Japan	22,000
1906	Valparaiso, Chile	1,500
1906	San Francisco, U.S.A.	700
1907	Kingston, Jamaica	1,400
1908	Messina, Italy	160,000
1915	Avezzano, Italy	30,000
1920	Kansu, China	200,000
1923	Tokyo, Japan	143,000
1930	Apennine Mountains, Italy	1,500
1932	Kansu, China	70,000
1935	Quetta, Baluchistan (Pakistan)	60,000
1939	Chile	30,000
1939	Erzincan, Turkey	40,000
1946	Alaska-Hawaii, U.S.A.	150
1948	Fuki, Japan	5,000
1949	Ecuador	6,000
1950	Assam, India	1,500
1953	Northwestern Turkey	1,200
1954	Northern Algeria	1,600
1956	Kabul, Afghanistan	2,000

Table 2-2 (continued)

YEAR	PLACE	DEATHS
1957	Northern Iran	2,500
1957	Western Iran	1,400
1957	Outer Mongolia	1,200
1960	Southern Chile	5,700
1960	Agadir, Morocco	12,000
1962	Northwestern Iran	12,000
1963	Barce, Libya	300
1963	Taiwan	100
1963	Skopje, Yugoslavia	1,000
1964	Anchorage, Alaska, U.S.A.	114
1967	Caracas, Venezuela	266
1971	San Fernando, Calif., U.S.A.	64
1972	Managua, Nicaragua	Several thousand

swaying ground motion may be felt up to 80 miles from the epicenter. Experience at the moderate 1971 San Fernando, California, earthquake showed that local intensities—when measured by strong-motion seismographs—may be as large in a moderate earthquake as in a great earthquake. However, in the great earthquake ground motion lasts longer and affects a larger area. The *intensity* of an earthquake's ground motion in a given locality, based on actual observations, is expressed by the Modified Mercalli Intensity Scale of 1931 (Table 2-3A).

It is well to remember that the Mercalli *intensity* scale is related to how an earthquake is felt, locally, and the damage done, while the Richter *magnitude* scale measures how great an earthquake is in terms of energy released.

SURFACE FAULTING A *fault* is a break in the earth's crust, sometimes several miles deep and up to hundreds of miles long, along which movement has taken place.

In a moderate earthquake, fault rupture along a rough plane in rock at an average depth of 5 to 10 kilometers may or may not extend to the surface, but it frequently does in shallow-focus earthquakes. Surface faulting develops *scarps* (steps), *graben* (trenches), fractures, and *pressure ridges* (looking like giant "mole tracks" or furrows). Spasmodic *creep* (slippage) occurs along many active faults, with and without earthquakes. In California—one of the most active earthquake areas in the world—all great earthquakes and many moderate earthquakes have been accompanied by surface fault breaks. In San Francisco, 1906, maximum horizontal displacement was 20 feet, with the east block moving south; the 1952 Arvin-Tehachapi, California, earthquake was accompanied by an upward thrusting movement of about 2 feet, and the block across the fault opposite the observer moved horizontally about 2 feet to the left. At San Fernando, 1971, the movement was similar to that in the Arvin-Tehachapi earthquake but was about 6 feet up and 6 feet horizontally to the left. Often complex fault fracturing occurs within a $\frac{1}{2}$-mile-wide zone

Table 2-3   How big is an earthquake?—Two scales

A. MODIFIED MERCALLI INTENSITY SCALE OF 1931* (1956 VERSION)†

 I. Not felt. Marginal and long-period effects of large earthquakes.
 II. Felt by persons at rest, on upper floors, or favorably placed.
 III. Felt indoors. Hanging objects swing. Vibration like passing of light trucks. Duration estimated. May not be recognized as an earthquake.
 IV. Hanging objects swing. Vibration like passing of heavy trucks, or sensation of a jolt like a heavy ball striking the walls. Standing motor cars rock. Windows, dishes, doors rattle. Glasses clink. Crockery clashes. In the upper range of IV wooden walls and frame creak.
 V. Felt outdoors; direction estimated. Sleepers wakened. Liquids disturbed, some spilled. Small unstable objects displaced or upset. Doors swing, close, open. Shutters, pictures move. Pendulum clocks stop, start, change rate.
 VI. Felt by all. Many frightened and run outdoors. Persons walk unsteadily. Windows, dishes, glassware broken. Knickknacks, books, etc., off shelves. Pictures off walls. Furniture moved or overturned. Weak plaster and masonry D‡ cracked. Small bells ring (church, school). Trees, bushes shaken visibly, or heard to rustle.
 VII. Difficult to stand. Noticed by drivers of motor cars. Hanging objects quiver. Furniture broken. Damage to masonry D, including cracks. Weak chimneys broken at roof line. Fall of plaster, loose bricks, stones, tiles, cornices, also unbraced parapets and architectural ornaments. Some cracks in masonry C. Waves on ponds; water turbid with mud. Small slides and caving in along sand or gravel banks. Large bells ring. Concrete irrigation ditches damaged.
 VIII. Steering of motor cars affected. Damage to masonry C; partial collapse. Some damage to masonry B; none to masonry A. Fall of stucco and some masonry walls. Twisting, fall of chimneys, factory stacks, monuments, towers, elevated tanks. Frame houses moved on foundations if not bolted down; loose panel walls thrown out. Decayed piling broken off. Branches broken from trees. Changes in flow or temperature of springs and wells. Cracks in wet ground and on steep slopes.
 IX. General panic. Masonry D destroyed; masonry C heavily damaged, sometimes with complete collapse; masonry B seriously damaged. General damage to foundations. Frame structures, if not bolted, shifted off foundations. Frames racked. Serious damage to reservoirs. Underground pipes broken. Conspicuous cracks in ground. In alluviated areas sand and mud ejected, earthquake fountains, sand craters.
 X. Most masonry and frame structures destroyed with their foundations. Some well-built wooden structures and bridges destroyed. Serious damage to dams, dikes, embankments. Large landslides. Water thrown on banks of canals, rivers, lakes, etc. Sand and mud shifted horizontally on beaches and flat land. Rails bent slightly.
 XI. Rails bent greatly. Underground pipelines completely out of service.
 XII. Damage nearly total. Large rock masses displaced. Lines of sight and level distorted. Objects thrown into the air.

*Original 1931 version in H. O. Wood, and F. Neumann, 1931, Modified Mercalli intensity scale of 1931, *Seismological Society of America Bulletin*, vol. 53, no. 5, pp. 979–987.

†1956 version prepared by Charles F. Richter, in 1958, *Elementary seismology*, W. H. Freeman & Co., San Francisco, pp. 137–138.

‡Masonry A, B, C, D. To avoid ambiguity of language, the quality of masonry, brick, or otherwise, is specified by the following lettering.

Table 2-3   (continued)

A. MODIFIED MERCALLI INTENSITY SCALE OF 1931,* (1956 VERSION)†

Masonry A. Good workmanship, mortar, and design; reinforced, especially laterally, and bound together by using steel, concrete, etc.; designed to resist lateral forces.
Masonry B. Good workmanship and mortar; reinforced, but not designed in detail to resist lateral forces.
Masonry C. Ordinary workmanship and mortar; no extreme weaknesses like failing to tie in at corners, but neither reinforced nor designed against horizontal forces.
Masonry D. Weak materials, such as adobe; poor mortar; low standards of workmanship; weak horizontally.

B. RICHTER MAGNITUDE

In 1935, Dr. Charles F. Richter of the California Institute of Technology devised a scale to indicate the "size" of an earthquake from the measured amplitude of an earthquake wave recorded on a *seismograph* (Chapter 11). The Richter magnitude, or just *magnitude* (M), is related to the total energy of the earthquake measured. This results in an open-ended scale based on energy released at the source and should be the same for a given earthquake, wherever measured. Near its epicenter an earthquake of M = 2 is the smallest felt, earthquakes of M = 4.5 to 5 may cause local damage, magnitudes of 7 or more are associated with "major" earthquakes, and those of 7.75 and over, with "great" earthquakes.

On this scale, the earthquake at San Fernando, California, in 1971 with M = 6.4 was a "moderate" one, the Arvin-Tehachapi, California, earthquake of M = 7.7 was a "major" one, and the Alaskan earthquake of 1964 at M = 8.4 was a "great" earthquake. Because of the way the scale is set up and its relation to energy, each higher number means that the earthquake is about 30 to 35 times as great as the next number below. For example, a magnitude 6 earthquake would involve roughly 30 to 35 times as much energy as a magnitude 5 earthquake. Thus the Alaskan earthquake was about 1,000 times as great as the San Fernando earthquake. The greatest known earthquake had a magnitude of about 8.9 on the Richter scale (Lisbon, 1755; see Chapter 12). Fortunately for the safety of all of us, minor earthquakes less than M = 2 are thousands of times more frequent than the great earthquakes.

---

with the dislocation of all surface features, including drainage and groundwater.

GROUND FAILURE   Ground disturbances and failures accompanying earthquakes include, particularly: landslides, fracturing, fissuring, slumping, "liquefaction" of fine sand layers (the flowing of water-saturated sediments), soil compaction, subsidence, uplift, and tilting.

Mass movements of loose rock, soil, and water-saturated, weathered materials are major effects in all earthquakes large enough to be felt. In hilly and steep areas all main roads may be closed for hours or days. Fine-grained sediments which are water-saturated may "liquefy," that is, lose all strength and flow in a thick mush. Sand boils and mud "volcanoes" (due to rising liquefied sediments) often accompany liquefaction. In the Niigata, Japan, earthquake, 1964, this happened under some multistory buildings. The buildings were well constructed and did not break up, but the soil beneath them liquefied and flowed out and the buildings slowly turned over on their sides. Some frightened people on the roof of one building hung on until the building settled and then walked down its side!

FRACTURING, FISSURING   Ground shaking, settling, compaction of earth, and sliding produce irregular fractures and fissures from inches to many feet long. Such fractures may displace earth and soil in a way similar to faults. Fractures are rare in solid rock, but are most significant in alluvium, soil, and weathered rock. Extensive pavement and curb rippling and fracturing may take place.

COMPACTION, SUBSIDENCE, UPLIFT   Compaction of soils and alluvium often takes place due, particularly, to shaking. Subsidence—lowering of the ground surface—may occur over areas a few feet across up to thousands of square miles, as in Alaska in 1964. Similarly, uplift may occur on a grand scale as it did also in Alaska. Of course, uplift and subsidence of the land need not be, and often are not, accompanied by earthquakes.

SEISMIC SEA WAVES AND SEICHES   The seismic sea wave, or *tsunami* ("tidal wave"), is a wave which is caused by earth movements on the sea floor or by submarine landslides. The wave may move at 300 to 400 miles per hour, with wave lengths from wave crest to wave crest of many miles in open water. Approaching shore, water may pile up to 50 or more feet in height. At Hilo, Hawaii, in 1946, a seismic sea wave 27 feet high moved across the town. At Crescent City, California, in 1964, the maximum wave height in the tsunamis following the Alaskan earthquake was about 24 feet. The U.S. Coast and Geodetic Survey operates such an efficient warning system that there is little reason for a person to be drowned by a seismic sea wave; yet, strangely enough, people do not always heed the warnings, and lives are lost.

Seiches, or periodic oscillation ("sloshing") of bodies of water such as ponds, lakes, and bays occur in moderate-to-great earthquakes and may raise and lower a water surface by inches to several feet. They occur as much as several thousand miles from a great earthquake.

So, How Do We Evaluate Earthquake Risk?   This involves prediction of earthquakes, time, place, and intensity (Chapter 12). We can do pretty well on this as long as we do not get too specific. We know, in general, *where* most earthquakes occur (Chapter 3). Of the world's damaging earthquakes 80 percent occur in a belt around the Pacific Ocean basin and 17 percent occur along the young mountain belt that trends through the East Indies, the Himalaya Mountains, and the Mediterranean Sea. Stay clear of these narrow areas and your risk of life and property is minimal! Yet, some of the world's great earthquakes have happened in the "safe" areas of the earth's surface: Mississippi Valley 1811 and 1812 and Charleston, South Carolina, 1886, are examples.

Our greatest clue to damage prediction, or earthquake risk, is earthquake history. An area of large population, with a history of frequent and violent earthquakes is most vulnerable! Dr. S. T. Algermissen (1969) of the National Oceanic and Atmospheric Administration has based his "Seismic risk map of the United States" on (1) earthquake history, (2) release of earthquake strain (distortion of rock under different pressures), and (3) the association of patterns of release of strain (an elastic "snapping back") with geologic features such as active faults and geologically young mountain systems.

California, our most populous state, has had more damaging earthquakes than any other. California is certainly earthquake country! In 200 years of records, the state has had 3 truly *great* earthquakes (like San Francisco, 1906), over 12 *major* earthquakes (like Arvin-Tehachapi, 1952), and over 60 *moderate*, but potentially damaging shocks (like Long Beach, 1933, and San Fernando, 1971). Should we move out? To perhaps be killed in a Kansas tornado, a Gulf Coast hurricane, or a Mississippi River flood? Of course not! Obviously, we *take measures*: we study earthquakes—their causes and characteristics—to learn as much as possible about this part of our environment; we build to resist earthquake forces; and we take steps to improve our measures for disaster preparedness and for postdisaster recovery.

RISKS OF VOLCANIC ERUPTIONS
In some ways the risks of volcanic eruptions are a little more apparent than earthquake risks. No one would pitch a tent on the floor of Halemaumau, the active pit crater of Kilauea in the Hawaiian Islands, nor occupy the hot crater of Mount Etna in Sicily! But how about the "dormant" and "extinct" volcanoes—like Krakatoa before 1883, or Mount Shasta in California since 1786, or Mount Pelée in the West Indies before 1902?

Ever since civilized people have been on the earth, they have been attracted to the rich soils of volcanic areas, the beauty of volcanic cones, and the gently sloping uplands at the bases of volcanic mountains.

The long and lurid history of Mount Vesuvius, Italy, is one of the most instructive of the eruptive actions of a great composite volcano. From the earliest occupation of southern Italy by the Greeks, centuries B.C., the ancestral Vesuvius ("Monte Somma") was quiet. It had the typical volcano form of a truncated cone, and the steep-sided summit crater at elevation 4,000 feet was overgrown with wild vines and trees. High on its flanks the fertile soil was richly cultivated and around the mountain lived a dense population. A series of minor earthquakes began in 63 A.D., and then in 79 A.D. came sudden and violent eruptions of water vapor, sulfurous gases, volcanic dust, ash, and larger rock fragments. Ash buried the town of Pompeii at the volcano's base, and hot mudflows engulfed Herculaneum as deep as 50 feet. Most inhabitants escaped, but not all; some were suffocated by ash and poisonous gases. Irregular periods of eruption occurred until 1138, followed by a period of no activity for 168 years. During this time people again forgot about the nature of the mountain and cultivated their fields high on its slopes. Again, eruptions from an "extinct" Vesuvius killed many people in 1631. Since 1631, eruptions have been intermittent, with a great one in 1872, and there has been almost continuous activity since 1906.

What happens in volcanic eruptions that make them so hazardous? *Glowing clouds*, consisting of dust, ash, rock fragments, water vapor, and sulfurous and other poisonous gases may form on the upper slopes of a volcano and move down at velocities up to 70 miles per hour, or more. Internal temperature of such dense clouds may be several hundreds of degrees Celsius. The city of St. Pierre in the West Indies was destroyed by such "glowing clouds" in 1902, killing about 40,000 people.

Lava flows may originate in the crater of a volcano, erupt from fissures on its flanks, or from fissures apart from any volcanic center. Lava flows follow preexisting valleys and as they move crust over and travel more and more slowly, at a rate of only a few feet per hour, but newly formed erupted molten lava may flow like water at several miles per hour. Usually, people can get out of their way, and flows can sometimes be diverted or temporarily slowed by man but cannot be stopped. Molten lava is also erupted explosively in masses of various sizes, as in Hawaii where blobs of magma are thrown as high as hundreds of feet into the air.

Volcanic ash and dust, consisting of solid rock and porous pumice, may be erupted in great volumes and may be transported in the atmosphere for thousands of miles. Ash falls may blanket thousands of square miles of the landscape. Clouds of volcanic ash are blinding, choking, and poisonous. The only human casualty in the 1973 ash eruptions of Kirkjufell on the Island of Heimaey in Iceland was a man who went into a cellar where heavy, poisonous gases had settled. Ash falls reduce visibility, kill vegetation, contaminate water, block pipes, and overload roofs.

Mudflows are often formed on the slopes of volcanoes where volcanic ash, dust, and larger fragments become saturated with water from rainfall or melting snow. Water is always present in great quantities in volcanic eruptions. Mudflows may be highly fluid and may flow for miles down mountain valleys.

Geologists of the U.S. Geological Survey, who are monitoring the activities of the Hawaiian volcanoes and of the chain of Cascade volcanoes that extends northerly from Lassen Peak in northern California to Mount Baker in northern Washington, classify mudflows and ash eruptions as the most potentially hazardous in the Cascades, and of course, lava flows present the volcanic hazard in Hawaii. The following quotation from U.S. Geological Survey geologists Crandell and Waldron (1969) gives us an idea of what has happened at Mount Rainier in the Cascades and what could happen:

At Mount Rainier, Washington, within the last 10,000 years there have been at least 55 large mudflows, several hot avalanches of rock debris, at least one period of lava flows, and at least 12 eruptions of volcanic ash. The last major eruption was about 2,000 years ago; it involved an eruption of lava and of pumice, and there were also several large mudflows. Within historic time, many eruptions on a minor scale were recorded in the 1800's, but only one produced pumice. If we assume that Rainier will continue to behave

Figure 2-2 Mt. Rainier, one of the greatest of the Cascade composite volcanoes, 14,410 feet high and a noted landmark southeast of Tacoma, Washington. Rainier last erupted in 1882. Like many volcanoes of its type, the position of its vent has shifted from time to time during its million-year history. Note the beautiful, crevassed Winthrop Glacier. We have discussed the hazards of Mr. Rainier and its monitoring by the U.S. Geological Survey. Its eruptions could endanger Tacoma and Seattle. (*Austin Post photo, U.S. Geological Survey.*)

as it has during the past 10,000 years, the principal hazard will be from mudflows down valley floors. These might consist of a few million cubic yards of mud and be confined to the valley floors very close to the volcano, but there is also a possibility of a huge mudflow, like the Osceola, which covered the present site of Enumclaw. The Osceola mudflow occurred about 5,000 years ago. It contained a little more than $2\frac{1}{2}$ billion cubic yards, that is, just a little more than half a cubic mile of material. It covered an area of about 125 square miles in the Puget Sound lowland where at least 30,000 people now live.

Crandell and Waldron speculate:

Consider the unfortunate Indian who was standing at the townsite of Enumclaw . . . about 5,000 years ago. He was probably looking in wonder

.at the clouds of steam and ash rising from mighty Tahoma, the mountain he called God, and which we call Mount Rainier. Although he probably felt safe at his distance of 25 airline miles from the volcano, he didn't realize that a wall of mud hundreds of feet deep was rushing down the White River Valley toward him. When he first saw the mudflow, it was still a mile away, but it was moving about 20 miles an hour. What do you suppose the reaction would be today of the present citizens of Enumclaw in a similar circumstance? Probably the same as the Indian's—run like hell!

Do *you* think that Mount Rainier is extinct, dormant, or active?

SUMMARY

What can you add to the list of historic disasters in Table 2-1? How important have earthquakes and volcanoes been in the world's great disasters?

The question of risk of earthquakes and volcanic eruptions is an extremely important and practical one. It involves social science, economics, and engineering, as well as geology. Take earthquake country like California, for example. Should we plan for future earthquakes and volcanic eruptions? If so, how much should our expenditures in money and manpower be *now*, to reduce future losses? Risk is an excellent subject for group discussion, involving, as it does, many disciplines—scientific, technical, and social. See Chapter 14 for further ideas related to risk and what can be done about volcanic eruptions and earthquakes.

To test your knowledge of the subjects in Chapter 2: (1) add to the things that can happen in moderate and great earthquakes and (2) discuss fully the differences between *intensity* and *magnitude* of an earthquake. Which of these two, for instance, is more important from the standpoint of safety of buildings?

In your part of the world, which is greater, the risk of earthquakes or the risk of volcanic eruptions? Why do you think so? Or are you in an area where neither volcanoes nor earthquakes are a hazard?

THREE

EARTHQUAKES

Where on earth do earthquakes occur? First, we must answer: Everywhere, anywhere! But if we look at a worldwide plot of earthquake epicenters (Figure 3-1) it is immediately apparent that the vast majority of earthquakes occur in three narrow belts. In Chapter 2 it was noted that 80 percent are found around the margin of the Pacific Ocean basin. The Aleutian Islands and Alaskan Peninsula; the coasts of southeastern Alaska and western North America, swinging through the West Indies and South America; New Zealand, the East Indies, the Philippines, Japanese Islands, and Kurile Islands, joining the Aleutian Islands in the northwestern part of the Pacific; this is the zone of great concentrations of earthquakes. A somewhat more diffuse zone of earthquakes—comprising about 17 percent—merges with the Pacific belt in the East Indies and extends northward and westward through the Himalaya Mountains, the Carpathian Mountains, and the Mediterranean Sea.

Besides the circum-Pacific and Mediterranean-Himalaya belts (of earthquakes), there is a third linear pattern of thin, narrow zones of earthquakes (Figure 3-2). One follows along the center of the mid-Atlantic Ocean, swinging southward from Iceland to stay midway between North America and Europe, and midway between South America and Africa. A similar, more-or-less continuous oceanic belt of earthquakes extends from the South Atlantic Ocean across the South Pacific and northward into the Indian Ocean, and a

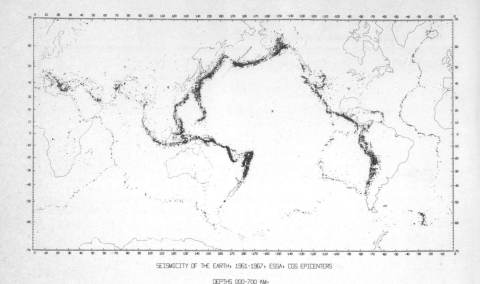

SEISMICITY OF THE EARTH, 1961-1967, ESSA, CGS EPICENTERS

DEPTHS 000-700 KM.

Figure 3-1 This map of the world, from the National Oceanic and Atmospheric Administration, shows the distribution of earthquakes over the earth for the years 1961–1967. Each earthquake epicenter is shown by a dot to represent a shock of magnitude 5 or greater. Depths of foci include the whole range from the near-surface to 700 kilometers. Note how the margins of the great tectonic plates, the midoceanic ridges, and the active subduction zones are outlined by earthquakes.

The worldwide pattern of geologically recent volcanoes is quite similar to this earthquake pattern.

semicircular belt swings westward from southern South America and northward to Central America. An East African belt heads northward from continental East Africa into the Red Sea and Dead Sea to merge into the Mediterranean belt of earthquakes.

The midoceanic and the East African belts account for most of the remaining 3 percent of the world's earthquakes, but there remain some earthquakes which have occurred entirely outside the mentioned earthquake belts, as, for example, in the eastern United States and southern interior Asia.

Most of the world's earthquakes are "shallow focus"; that is, they appear to originate at foci less than 70 kilometers deep. They have the distribution we have been talking about. However, there are deep-focus earthquakes, originating at depths between 300 and 700 kilometers; and also intermediate-focus earthquakes between 70 and 300 kilometers deep. They are much more limited in their distribution than are the shallow-focus earthquakes. Most of the world's earthquakes over 100 kilometers deep are along portions of the Pacific belt, particularly along the west coasts of Central and South America; the Fiji-Tonga islands north of New Zealand and the East Indies and island arcs of the east coast of Asia; and the Aleutian arc. Once again, there are exceptions to this generalization, but they are few.

VOLCANOES

There are some 600 to 800 active volcanoes on the surface of the earth today. Don't pin us down too closely; we have already found that the distinction between "extinct," "dormant," or "active" is a tenuous one. There have been 3,294 eruptions recorded at 483 volcanoes since 1700.

The margin of the Pacific basin is a "rim of fire" where over 75 percent of the world's active volcanoes are located. This belt coincides roughly with the circum-Pacific belt of earthquakes. However, the volcanic belts are not as continuous as the earthquake belts. Quite a long gap exists, for example, between recent volcanic cones in the Mojave Desert and Salton Sea basin in California and the great volcanoes near Mexico City. The Mediterranean Sea-to-East Indies earthquake belt is not continuously volcanic, but is marked by clusters of active volcanoes in the Mediterranean, some in the Caucasus, and then many in the East Indies. There are none in between, across Turkey and the Himalayas. Many volcanic eruptions—but by no means all—are preceded by swarms of small to moderate earthquakes, but no *great* earthquake has ever been of volcanic origin as far as we know. Suddenly increased volcanic action has accompanied and followed earthquakes in

Figure 3-2 Historic earthquakes in the United States through 1970, magnitude 5 and over. Note the concentrations in the far west, the east, and the Mississippi Valley around southern Illinois. The small numbers indicate the numbers of earthquakes at the same epicenter. Tie in specific epicenters with the text accounts. (*National Oceanic and Atmospheric Administration, Earthquake history of the United States, Publication 41-1.*)

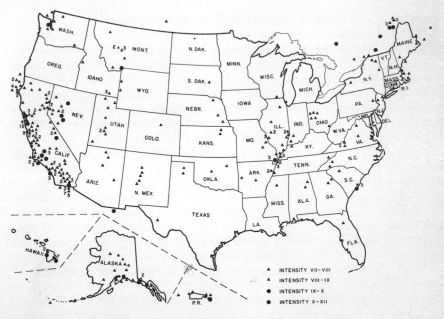

Central America and in Chile, for example, but this has been rather exceptional activity.

There is an association of active volcanoes with the East African fault, or "rift" valleys, and along the midoceanic ridges, particularly along the Mid-Atlantic Ridge—on Iceland near the north end of the ridge, for example. But there are thousands of miles of the midoceanic ridges where fluid black lava upwells quietly along fissures without accompanying active volcanoes.

Outside the defined belts of active volcanoes, we know that all the islands of the Pacific Ocean are tops of volcanoes of recent origin. The Hawaiian Islands are over a volcanic "hot spot" several million years old, and some of the world's largest and most active shield volcanoes make up the Island of Hawaii. In the Pacific basin the Galapagos Islands and Samoa are also marked by active volcanoes.

Where are there no active volcanoes? The great and ancient (Precambrian) *continental shield* areas—North American, Australian, African, Scandinavian—while once sites of active volcanism and earthquakes, are apparently free of both active volcanoes and earthquakes. Yet the ancient Brazilian continental shield was fissured and vast quantities of lava flooded the area in Cretaceous time.

Scientists are beginning to learn something about the distribution of earthquakes and volcanoes. In the next section of this book we shall look at a fascinating new approach to the problems of distribution of the world's earthquakes and volcanoes.

THE GRAND PICTURE: MOVING CRUSTAL PLATES AND THEIR JUNCTURES

In late 1963, fishermen were awed, frightened, and fascinated by the sudden, violent boiling of the sea a few miles off the coast of Iceland. Shortly, columns of "smoke," steam, and flame shot thousands of feet into the air, followed by upbuilding of an island of steaming black rock and molten orange and yellow lava. A new island—Surtsey—named, appropriately enough, after the Norse fire giant *Surtur*, had literally burst from the Atlantic. Here was new land that the world had never seen before!

In early 1963 a short paper was published by a Canadian scientist, J. Tuzo Wilson, which triggered a revolution in geological thinking. This was an event just as unsettling to earth scientists as was the birth of Surtsey to the Icelandic fisherman! Wilson's hypothesis of sea-floor spreading and continental drift was by far the more important event, for a decade of impressive, worldwide evidence has just about elevated this "working hypothesis" to a *theory*—a verified hypothesis—fundamental to explanation of some of the earth's greatest features, including volcanoes and earthquakes.

Why mention these two events of 1963 in the same breath? In a moment, we shall see.

Continental drift was not a new idea. Centuries ago thinkers of the times

(Sir Francis Bacon, in 1620, for instance) noticed that the east coast of South America and a large part of the west coast of Africa seemed to be a perfect fit. Had these continents drifted apart through the geologic ages? Proof was lacking. In 1912 Alfred Wegener, a German meteorologist, proposed that the continents had once all been one and that they had split and drifted apart. Wegener's ideas practically died, scientifically, particularly because they could not be proved.

Then, in 1960 the noted geologist Harry H. Hess, Professor of Geology at Princeton University, offered a hypothesis as "geopoetry." He said that the sea floors split open along the crests of mountainous *midocean ridges*, and that black lava wells up in the central crack and spreads out to form new sea floor on both sides of the ridges. This is precisely what we saw happening in 1963 at Surtsey and in 1973 at Heimaey—another isle off Iceland. In fact, the island of Iceland lies directly in the Mid-Atlantic Ridge and is itself a very young volcanic island formed by upwelling lava from the great rift zone along the midoceanic ridge. During the present century, Icelanders have experienced 14 eruptions such as those of Surtsey and Heimaey as the island has split apart.

Thus, the violent explosions of Surtsey to Heimaey, 1963 to 1973, have built new land on the earth, just as the revolution in geologic thinking called *plate tectonics*—involving sea-floor spreading and moving continental and oceanic plates—is building a grand new theory leading to understanding of the earth's most fundamental geologic features!

The new study of plate tectonics—developing in great strides since the late 1960s—involves the concept that the earth's crust, or *lithosphere*, is made up of about seven huge, more-or-less rigid, but elastic, plates (Figure 3-3) about 75 to 100 kilometers thick, plus about twenty smaller plates, all of which move—"drift"—over a plastic layer, called the *aesthenosphere*, which is located between depths of about 100 to 200 kilometers. Fifty years ago Beno Gutenberg, one of the world's great seismologists, noted that earthquake waves move more slowly in the 100- to 200-kilometer layer than elsewhere. He interpreted this low-velocity zone in terms of a plastic, or perhaps even partly liquid, layer. The driving mechanism for the plates may be convection; that is, currents in hot, plastic materials and liquid magma may move upward and outward in the aesthenosphere, away from spreading centers, carrying the plates with them, and finally downward again under deep trenches at the margins of eastern Asia, the Aleutians, and the west coast of South America (Figure 3-3).

The lithospheric plates have three kinds of boundaries: (1) oceanic plates spread apart at the great cracks in the midoceanic ridges and magma wells up in the cracks to form new crust which then moves away from the ridges at rates of a few centimeters a year; (2) the new oceanic crust formed moves outward until eventually it dives down beneath a continental margin; and (3) junctures, either on land or on the sea floor, where the plates slide horizontally past each other along great faults. Note that the midoceanic ridge boundaries are *spreading centers*, where plates are formed and move apart. Boundaries where plates move down beneath continental margins are *subduction zones*—(Figure 3-4)—places where crust is being consumed and destroyed and the earth's surface is being shortened. At the *fault boundaries*, where plates are sliding past each other, there is neither spreading nor shortening of the earth's crust. There are also places where two moving continental plates come into contact with each other. A notable example is the relative northward movement of the subcontinent of India, which is colliding with the main continent of Asia to form the Himalaya Mountains.

Now, at last, we are getting at the causes of things! Volcanic action, faulting causing earthquakes, and mountain building (which we cannot expand on in this book on volcanoes and earthquakes) are not isolated phenomena; they are all closely and logically related. The plate junctures are where the action is in terms of volcanic activity, earthquakes, and mountain building.

By no means are the highlights of plate tectonics, which we have outlined here, universally accepted by geological scientists as "truth." A scientific controversy rages between the majority who tend to accept plate tectonic theory and a highly competent minority who see great fallacy in it. This is a most healthy and stimulating dispute, for it fosters detailed, critical

Figure 3-3 The earth's moving crustal plates. The great oceanic plates—like the Pacific plate—appear to move faster than the continental plates—like the American—with respect to the interior of the earth. The oceanic plates move an average of about 10 centimeters (4 inches) a year, whereas the continental plates appear to move an average of 2 centimeters a year. Along the midoceanic ridges note that the arrows indicate that the adjacent plates are moving away from each other; in areas like the Aleutian Trench and Japanese trench the oceanic plate is sliding down under the edge of the continental plate; and in other places—as along California's San Andreas Fault—the theory is that the two plates are sliding past each other. (*California Geology, September 1973.*)

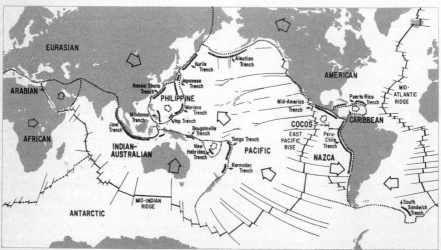

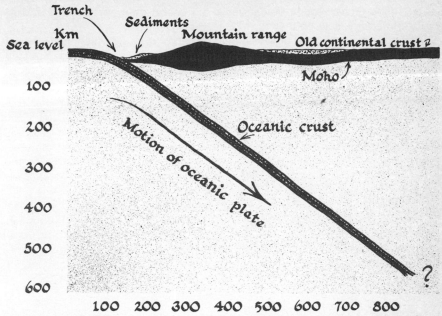

Figure 3-4 Subduction zone at a continental margin, an idealized model. This is a model of the sort of thing that plate tectonics theory says is happening at the continental margins of eastern Asia and the Aleutian Islands region. Oceanic crust is being pushed downward under the continental margin, thus developing a trench back of an island arc and bowing up a mountain range continentward from the trench. (*Modified from various sources.*)

study of the evidence and is sure to lead to rapid increases in our knowledge of the fundamental processes that fashion our earth!

SUMMARY

In Chapter 3, we attempt to look briefly at modern theories on the fundamental causes of earthquakes and volcanoes. The theory of plate tectonics—the grand picture of moving crustal plates and their junctures—is revolutionizing geologic thinking. No other theory has offered such fascinating possibilities in terms of understanding such great geologic phenomena as volcanoes and the faulting that causes earthquakes.

First, we look at worldwide patterns of historic earthquakes and active volcanoes and we note impressive tie-ins with plate boundaries and oceanic spreading centers. In terms of volcanic activity, faulting and earthquakes, and mountain building, the plate junctures are where the action is.

How, then, do we account for earthquakes deep within the ancient geologic formations of a continental interior, far from a known plate juncture? *Can* we account for them in terms of plate tectonic theory? What about geologically young volcanoes a thousand miles or more inland in North America? How do they fit in?

Plate tectonics opens up a vast field of geologic study which may interest you—and there is now a large literature on this subject. Warning: You will find that you'll need to go more and more deeply into geological and other sciences if you are to develop any real understanding of the strengths and weaknesses of this imaginative theory.

FOUR

VOLCANIC ERUPTIONS: THE MAKING OF VOLCANIC ROCKS

Vulcan, the god of fire, worked intermittently at his roaring, fiery forge on an island in the Mediterranean Sea.

Thus, the ancient Romans explained the unpredictable, frequent, and terrifying volcanic eruptions of their world. Today we hardly credit the whims of the gods with these things, but Vulcan's island—Vulcano—exists off the coast of Sicily and the name survives in such terms as *volcano, volcanic,* and *volcanism.*

The very definition of volcano includes the thought of eruption. All volcanoes erupt at one time or another, and all kinds of volcanic activity (volcanism) bring heat to the surface of the earth.

When you think of a volcano you may think of a *vent,* or opening, from which hot materials are erupted, or you may think of the peak or accumulation of volcanic rock built up by repeated eruptions. You are right in both ideas. Volcanoes and volcanism are, by definition, surface, or near-surface, phenomena; these terms do not apply when magma crystallizes well below the surface of the earth.

VOLCANIC LANDFORMS

Active and geologically young volcanoes provide some of the most majestic and beautiful of all mountains. Typical volcanic cones with their symmetrical forms and concave slopes, becoming steeper and steeper toward their

Figure 4-1 Looking south at Mount Shasta (left) and Shastina, beautiful composite volcanoes of the Cascade Range in northern California. Geology and history suggest that the active vent shifted from Shasta to Shastina and then back to Mount Shasta for the latest eruption in 1786. (*Scratchboard drawing by Peter H. Oakeshott.*)

summit craters, offer a scenic beauty whose origin cannot be mistaken. Built of lava flows and fragments of volcanic rock from repeated violent eruptions, the *composite* volcanoes, such as snow-capped Fujiyama (12,188 feet in elevation) in Japan; the double peak of 14,162-foot Mount Shasta and its satellite, Shastina (Figure 4-1), in northern California; the extraordinarily symmetrical Mayon Volcano in the Philippines; Mount Rainier (14,410 feet) in the state of Washington; and the snow-sheathed Shisaldin Volcano (9,372 feet) in the Aleutian Islands are certainly among nature's most pleasing and striking scenes. The historically famous Mount Vesuvius in Italy and Mount Etna in Sicily are great, active, composite volcanoes.

With much the same conical form, but usually smaller and with steeper slopes and relatively larger craters, are the *cinder cones*, built almost entirely of fragments of volcanic rock. Examples are the 1,000-foot-high Paricutin in Mexico which first erupted in 1943, 200-foot-high Amboy Crater in southern California, the multiple little cinder cones in the summit crater of Mauna Kea on the island of Hawaii, and the small 500-year-old Cinder Cone near Lassen Peak in northern California.

Although we think of the cinder cones and composite volcanoes as the "typical" volcanic landforms, many volcanoes are nearly circular rounded *domes* or are made up of domes within craters. These form from stubby upwellings of viscous lava which is high in silica and does not flow far. Among the most perfect examples are the Mono Craters in eastern California, consisting mostly of *obsidian* (volcanic glass). They were formed as viscous obsidian plugs rose up through the floors of explosion pits. Thus, these domes grew from within. Other examples are Novarupta Dome (Figure 4-2*a* and *b*), Alaska; Showa-Shinzan Dome, Japan; and Santiaguito Dome in Guatemala. All these extend only a few hundred feet above the plateaus or crater floors on which they were built. In several, the upwelling plug or spine did not quite fill the crater, thus a moat (circular valley) is left between the spine and the walls of the crater.

The largest volcano in the world is 13,680-foot Mauna Loa, which dominates the island of Hawaii. It is a *shield* volcano, a low, flat dome 60 miles long by 30 miles wide, actually built up from the sea floor, which here is about 17,000 feet deep. The shield volcanoes are enormous and are built up of thousands of layers of highly fluid, low-silica lava. Lava *plateaus*—like the 150,000 square mile Columbia Plateau of the northwestern United States, the Deccan Plateau of India, and others—are built of similar lava which has erupted from *fissures*, or cracks in the earth to build up multiple flows totaling as much as 2,000 feet in depth in many places, and reaching maximum local depths of 4 kilometers, or almost $2\frac{1}{2}$ miles.

A volcano is readily eroded by wind, rain, running water, ice, and snow, with loose volcanic ash and rock fragments easily washed down the steep slopes. Most resistant to erosion and the last part of a volcano to remain is the hard, resistant plug (spine or *neck*) of rock that filled the pipelike conduit that carried magma from below up to the summit crater or vent. Agathla Butte, in the famous Monument Valley, Arizona, is a volcanic neck. Shiprock, in New Mexico, a vertical-sided plug of volcanic rock standing 1,600 feet above a plain, surrounded by radiating wall-like *dikes* (made by tabular injections of magma into rock), is a noted volcanic neck. These are two necks among about 150 in Arizona and New Mexico that mark the locations of a swarm of long-extinct volcanoes. Near San Luis Obispo, California, a row of about 14 steep, sharp, conical peaks, each several hundred feet high, is strung out along a northwest-trending fault or fracture zone in the southern Coast Ranges. The most northwesterly of these is Morro Rock standing prominently out of Morro Bay. These are the eroded remnants of early Miocene (Table 1-1) volcanoes. Morro Rock has been radiometrically dated at about 23 million years—a very tough, resistant volcanic neck!

We can hardly close this short sketch of volcanic landforms without mentioning the giant craters called *calderas*. They are formed from gigantic explosive eruptions, like the caldera of Krakatoa; or from the progressive collapse of the rims of craters as fluid lava (*magma*) is withdrawn from below, like the calderas of Mauna Loa and Kilauea. None is more beautiful than Crater Lake, Oregon. The site of Crater Lake was occupied a few thousand years ago by Mount Mazama, a composite volcano much like Mount Shasta is

(a)

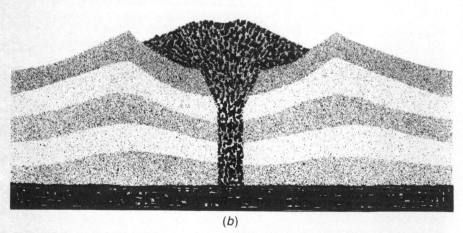

(b)

Figure 4-2(*a*) Novarupta Dome volcano, Katmai region, Alaska. This near-circular crater, about 800 feet across, grew by addition of layers of lava fanning upward and outward from within. (*b*) Cross section of Novarupta Dome. (*Scratchboard drawing by Peter H. Oakeshott from photos and diagrams by U.S. Geological Survey.*)

today. The summit of Mount Mazama collapsed and left a huge crater—a caldera—6 miles across. Due to the moist climate, a deep, clear-blue lake was formed; projecting above the lake is Wizard Island, a small cinder cone built up by the last eruptions within the caldera.

Landforms like these of the great volcanoes have short geological lives; they are soon (geologically speaking!) reduced by erosion and lose all semblance of their volcanic form. All the volcanoes we have named here reached their present form during the Quaternary Period, the last 3 million years of geologic time. Of course, there were ancestral volcanoes on the same sites in some cases.

WHERE DOES LAVA COME FROM AND HOW DOES IT MOVE?
The earth is a great mass of igneous rock which is distinctly layered. Studies of the passage of earthquake waves tell us that the earth has a high-density, solid core surrounded by a liquid outer core, which in turn is surrounded by the *mantle*, which is made up of successive layers of rock of decreasing density. Most interesting in our study of volcanoes and volcanism are the earth's *crust* and *outer mantle*, for it is in these layers that volcanic activity occurs.

The crust is quite variable in thickness but is relatively thin beneath the oceans and thick under the continents. Continental crust is roughly from 20 to 60 kilometers thick, averaging about 33 kilometers (20 miles) and with an average composition similar to that of rhyolite and granite. Oceanic crust averages about $5\frac{1}{2}$ kilometers thick and has the composition of basalt. The upper mantle probably consists of rock similar to a basalt, but with more magnesium and iron silicates.

Several years ago seismologists discovered that the velocity of earthquake waves was distinctly lowered as they passed through the upper mantle between depths of about 60 to 250 kilometers. This *low-velocity zone* is less rigid and less dense than the rock layers above it and below it and is probably close to the melting temperature of the rock. It is in the low-velocity zone and lower crust, between about 40 and 60 kilometers in depth, that remelting goes on to form bodies of magma, which may either solidify higher in the crust as bodies of igneous rock or reach the surface in volcanic activity.

Where does all the heat come from and why are pockets of rock melted to form magma chambers? We have only partial answers. Part of the earth's heat has been retained since its early molten history, and a large part of it continues to come from the process of radioactive decay of uranium, thorium, and other elements. Perhaps concentrations of these elements produce local hot spots, or local deformation and uplift of the crust may reduce pressures and cause melting; we do not know.

Once molten rock has been formed, its lower density in relation to surrounding rock causes it to begin to move upward under the influence of gravity. Gases within the magma give a lift, also, just as gas mixed with oil helps an oil well to flow.

WHAT DO VOLCANOES ERUPT AND WHY?
Vast amounts of magma do cool at depth within the earth's crust to form granite and other less abundant kinds of rock; such bodies are said to be

plutonic and the processes and activities are *plutonism*. *Igneous* is the inclusive term that covers all volcanism and plutonism and their products.

The examples discussed in Chapters 1 and 2 can be extended to impress us with the great diversity of volcanic landforms and volcanic activity or behavior, and the variety of products of volcanic eruptions. Volcanoes may be cones or domes, steep-sided or nearly flat, a few feet high or thousands of feet high, or volcanism may build up extensive plateaus. Eruptions may take place from central vents or along fissures; there may be prominent craters or explosion pits, or the craters may be filled by volcanic materials. Not infrequently, huge crater pits, or calderas, have formed by gigantic explosions and/or collapse as lava is withdrawn from below.

Is there any regular periodicity to volcanic eruptions? Not usually, although some volcanoes—like Kilauea—may erupt every few years. Most volcanoes—like Vesuvius—are intermittent in their activity, with long intervals of quiescence of several hundreds to perhaps thousands of years between eruptions. Eruptions may last hours, days, or years. Some volcanoes have historic records of eruptions over thousands of years—like Vesuvius and Etna; other volcanoes—like Paricutin in Mexico in 1943, and Surtsey in Iceland in 1963—we have seen start from scratch as entirely new volcanoes.

How long do volcanoes "live"? Probably some erupt a matter of days and become extinct. But, knowing that a volcano can be dormant for centuries and then erupt again, when can we be certain that a volcano has really died? Geologic evidence suggests that some volcanoes may well have started their activity in latest Tertiary or earliest Quaternary time—say, about 3 million years ago.

What do volcanoes erupt and why? Clearly, volcanoes erupt gases, liquids, and solids—usually all three—in highly varying proportions in different volcanoes and from time to time in the same volcano.

Gases By far the most abundant of all gases in all volcanic eruptions is water vapor (H_2O). There is usually about 3 to 10 times as much water, by weight, as carbon dioxide (CO_2), the next most abundant constituent of volcanic gases. Perhaps third in abundance are the sulfurous gases— molecular sulfur (S_2), sulfur dioxide (SO_2), and hydrogen sulfide (H_2S). Thus, the principal chemical elements present are hydrogen, oxygen, carbon, and sulfur.

Volcanic gases also contain traces of a number of other elements, often occurring as simple compounds. Among the elements often present in small proportions are nitrogen and argon (perhaps from the atmosphere), boron, chlorine, fluorine, and metallic elements, including copper, iron, mercury, and zinc. The presence of metallic elements is interesting, for many ore deposits seem to have been formed from solutions associated with late stages of igneous activity.

Throughout nearly all of the $4\frac{1}{2}$ billion years of geologic history volcanism has been a major process, building new rock at the surface of the earth and bringing vast quantities of gases to the surface. The waters on the earth and the earth's nitrogen-oxygen-water atmosphere are probably originally of volcanic origin.

At the highest temperatures of eruption (perhaps 1100–1200°C) some gases may exist as elements but will combine as temperatures fall. For example, burning hydrogen (H_2) has been noted in some very hot gases in Hawaiian eruptions. Hydrogen and oxygen, which may exist independently at high temperatures, combine to form water as the temperature falls. Sulfur, present at all temperatures, is probably mostly in the form of SO_2 at high temperatures and H_2S at low temperatures. Elemental chlorine (Cl) and fluorine (F) at high temperatures combine with hydrogen to form hydrochloric acid (HCl) and hydrofluoric acid (HF) at low temperatures. SO_2 tends to combine with oxygen and water to form sulfuric acid (H_2SO_4). Since HCl, HF, and H_2SO_4 are extremely strong acids, they never last long, but rapidly act on rocks to form new chemical compounds. Carbon monoxide (CO) existing at high temperatures combines with oxygen at lower temperatures to form CO_2. Further, CO_2 combines with H_2O to form carbonic acid, a weak acid but one which is very important in the weathering of rocks.

What proportion of the products of eruption are gases? At the height of a volcanic eruption gases probably make up about 0.5 to 1 percent of the material, by weight. As volcanic eruptions die out and a volcano becomes quiescent or dormant, lava and fragmental rock are no longer erupted, but liquid water and gases like CO_2, H_2S, and methane (CH_4) are present in hot springs and *fumaroles* ("smoke holes").

Lava By far the greatest volume of the materials that volcanoes erupt is lava. It originates in the lower crust and upper mantle of the earth in areas or pockets where rock melts to form magma. Magma rises to the surface of the earth, or nearly to the surface, where we change the name of the melt to *lava*. Lava is, of course, the same material as magma, but as the molten rock nears the surface, pressures are lowered and water and the other gases are largely lost.

What is lava made of? Mostly silicon dioxide (SiO_2), usually called *silica*. Nearly all lavas contain over 45 percent silica. Next in abundance to silica, in decreasing proportions in the melt, are oxides of aluminum (Al), iron (Fe), calcium (Ca), sodium (Na), potassium (K), magnesium (Mg), and some remaining water. All other constituents total only about $1\frac{1}{2}$ percent of lavas.

Rocks Lava "freezes" or solidifies to form volcanic rocks. In terms of their chemical composition, volcanic rocks—and the lavas from which they originate—are of three principal types: *rhyolite, andesite,* and *basalt.* Chemically, these are defined largely by their silica content. Rhyolitic lava is about three-fourths silica, andesitic lava about two-thirds silica, and basaltic lava about one-half silica. When rocks, or lava, are high in silica they are said to be *felsic*; those low in silica are *mafic.* Most lavas are in the basaltic to rhyolitic range, basalt being the most abundant of all volcanic materials.

The higher the silica content, the more likely that the lava will also be high in sodium and/or potassium. Low-silica volcanic materials are often higher in calcium, magnesium, and iron oxides. Because iron imparts a dark color and is heavy, the lower-silica lavas are likely to be dark in color (dark gray, dark green, or black) and to have a relatively high specific gravity.

Rocks are the solid materials that make up the fundamental units of the earth's crust. A *rock* is an aggregate of minerals and has a characteristic chemical composition, mineral composition, and texture.

Like people, rocks reflect their origin and environment. And because of the great variety of environments and conditions under which igneous rocks form, there has developed a complex nomenclature of hundreds of rock names. Almost every variant in composition, texture, and geographic location has a name. Fortunately, we can group the volcanic types into a minimum of significant species.

Texture refers to the size, shape, and arrangement of mineral grains within a rock. Texture depends on the history of formation of the rock, particularly on the rate of cooling of magma and lava, and on its chemical composition. Textures tell us much about the environmental history of rocks. Instantaneous chilling may develop a rock of *glassy* texture, that is, with no distinct mineral crystals. The relatively rapid cooling of magmas as they come to the surface of the earth favors the development of *fine-grained* textures composed of very small crystals. However, not all minerals crystallize out of a magma under the same conditions of pressure and temperature. Some mineral crystals form first; later, relatively rapid solidification of the whole mass forms solid rock. This may result in well-formed mineral crystals of larger size in a fine-grained or glassy matrix or *groundmass*. This texture is termed *porphyritic* and is common in lava flows, as well as in the shallow sheetlike intrusions which are injected across older layered rock (*dikes*) or are injected parallel to older rock layers (*sills*).

Now, since volcanic rocks consist of aggregates of minerals, we need to know something about the commonest rock-forming minerals.

The Rock-forming Minerals   Although there are probably over 2,000 mineral species, those minerals that form the great bulk of the igneous rocks are few in number. A *mineral* is a naturally occurring inorganic substance of characteristic chemical composition and crystal structure. Minerals show differences in color, luster (shine), hardness, specific gravity, streak (color of their powder), patterns of fracture and cleavage (splitting controlled by crystal structure), and crystal form.

All the commonest minerals of igneous rocks are *silicates*. What do we mean by that? First, we know that oxygen and silicon are overwhelmingly the most abundant elements in the rock-forming minerals, making up about three-quarters of their weight. These two elements have a strong chemical attraction for each other. Four oxygen atoms combine with one silicon atom in a pattern such that the oxygen atoms are at equal distances from the silicon atom to form the silicon-oxygen tetrahedron, written as SiO_4. This is the fundamental unit of construction of the silicate minerals.

Quartz (pure silica, SiO_2) is one of the commonest of minerals. It is usually colorless or white; it is very hard—harder than steel; and it breaks with an irregular, curved fracture like glass. It may show its characteristic crystal form—a six-sided prism topped by a six-sided pyramid. Quartz is an essential constituent of the high-silica rocks—rhyolite, rhyodacite, and dacite.

Feldspars is the name applied to a family of minerals that are made up of shared silica tetrahedrons in which aluminum takes the place of some of the silicon. The feldspars are aluminum silicates of potassium, sodium, and calcium. They are the commonest of all minerals and many volcanic rocks are composed of little else but feldspars and quartz. They are an essential constituent of volcanic rocks from rhyolite to basalt; K feldspars and Na feldspars predominate in the high-silica rocks, while Ca feldspars are more abundant in the low-silica rocks. They are white or grayish minerals and are hard, but not as hard as quartz. The fact that the feldspars split along two prominent crystal planes of weakness, resulting in two sets of flat, shiny surfaces called *cleavage planes*, helps in distinguishing them from quartz, which has no cleavage.

Micas are also a family of minerals made up of complex silicates. A colorless variety is called *muscovite* and a black or brown variety is *biotite*. The micas are very easily recognized because of their very perfect cleavage; they split into extremely thin, flat, and shiny plates. They are most often a minor constituent of the high-silica volcanic rocks.

Pyroxene and *hornblende* are common families of minerals. Both are complex silicates of varying composition which include the whole list of common elements. They have many different colors, but most common are black, brown, and green. Both form long prismatic crystals or needles in rock, but the pyroxenes show two good cleavage faces which form a right angle, while the hornblendes show two good cleavage faces which meet at angles of 120 or 60°. Hornblende is more common in the felsic volcanic rocks; pyroxene is more common in basalts.

Olivine, an iron magnesium silicate, is a hard, green mineral with no cleavage.

Structures in Volcanic Rocks Rapid cooling of lavas freezes a variety of structures into the volcanic rocks which are formed. These depend a lot on the chemical composition of the lava, the rate of cooling, and the water and gas content. *Vesicular* structures are formed when escaping gases leave holes or vesicles; later filling of these gas holes may result in agates or other attractive materials. Tubes and caverns are also common. For example, the lava flows at Kilauea, Hawaii, are highly porous and crusty, full of vesicles, caverns, tubes, and tunnels. Later lava flows often follow the tunnels and may not even appear on the surface. Lava tubes and tunnels are formed when the surface of a basalt flow highly charged with gas crystallizes and the still-molten lava within continues to move on. Such lava tunnels are a great tourist attraction in Hawaii, in the Lava Beds National Monument (Figure 4-3) in Siskiyou County, California, and in Hot Creek Valley in Shasta County, California. Sometimes, during eruptions, the tops of lava tubes collapse and lava erupts onto the surface to build up *spatter cones* a few feet high. Huge bubbles or blisters several feet or yards across, splitting as they cool, may develop on basalt flows.

Basaltic lava, emerging at temperatures of 800 to 1100°C, is highly fluid and may flow down a gentle slope for miles. Flows often develop smooth, ropy surfaces called *pahoehoe* after Hawaiian lava. Somewhat less com-

Figure 4-3 Dark entrance to a partially collapsed lava tube (or cave) in Lava Beds National Monument, Siskiyou County, California. This is one of nearly 300 tubes in the area. Such tubes form when the surface of a river of basaltic lava chills and the more slowly cooling interior continues to flow. The rock is Quaternary basalt. (*Charles W. Chesterman photo.*)

monly, the lava flows crust over to form a highly irregular, clinkery surface called *aa*. High-silica rhyolitic lava is much more viscous ("sticky") than basaltic lava and so tends to form short stubby flows and is more highly explosive, because the gases cannot escape as readily from the sticky lava. Rhyolitic lavas solidify at relatively high temperatures, and the contained gases may be held and released explosively. Beautiful rhyolite glass (obsidian) flows are strikingly developed at Glass Mountain in Siskiyou County in northern California. Thus, flow structures form in all sorts of cooling lavas.

Among the most spectacular of structures formed in cooling lava flows are *columnar joints. Joints* are cracks that appear in more-or-less regular patterns. Among the finest and most-visited exposures of columnar jointing are the Giant's Causeway in northern Ireland, the Devil's Postpile National Monument (Figure 4-4) in the heart of the high Sierra Nevada in California, and the Palisades of the valley of the Hudson River in New York. Four-to-six-sided columns developed in a uniformly cooling andesitic lava flow at the Devil's Postpile about 1 million years ago. The 600-foot-thick lava flow contracted about centers as it cooled, forming joints that make a polygonal pattern. The columns are from a few inches to several feet across, and some are about a hundred feet long. Always, the length of the columns is perpendicular to the cooling surface, that is, the tops and bottoms of the flows.

Explosive Volcanic Rocks   Extrusions of lava build new volcanic rock at the surface of the earth and volcanic gases add to the atmosphere and the waters around the earth.

In addition to vast quantities of molten rock, the more violent volcanic eruptions furnish solid rock fragments to the surface accumulations. Fragmental materials include pieces of the wall rock plucked out along the pipes and vents which bring lava to the surface in volcanic eruptions, crystallized pieces of magma, large blocks, and craggy and jumbled masses of collapsed spines which sometimes fill the craters of volcanoes.

It is the viscous, high-silica magmas which are most likely to trap gases under high pressure until violent explosions occur. Consequently, most of the *tephra* or *pyroclastics*—collective names given to the fragmental products of explosive volcanic eruption—have the composition of rhyolite. The

Figure 4-4 Jointing in Pleistocene lava flow, Devil's Postpile, San Joaquin River, Sierra Nevada. (*California Division of Mines and Geology photo.*)

finest tephra consists of dust and *ash*; *cinders* are vesicular fragments around 1 centimeter or so in diameter. *Lapilli* are pea-sized globules which chilled as they turned in the air during their eruption and fall to earth; *bombs* are head-sized rounded masses of similar origin. Pyroclastics are glassy because of almost instantaneous cooling. Obsidian is formed when magma congeals so quickly that it forms a solid solution; no mineral crystals have had time to develop. *Pumice* is a glassy froth, so light that a piece of it will float on water until its pore spaces become filled. On the island of Hawaii, and not uncommonly in other volcanic areas, one can find little bunches of finely spun glassy hair, called *Pele's hair*, produced by local eruptions of glassy froth.

Vast *ash flows*—both from central vents and long cracks or fissures—have built up ash fields over hundreds or thousands of square miles, consisting of sheets of tephra generated by the explosive eruption of intensely hot, churning mixtures of incandescent dust, ash, cinders, and pumice. About 33 million years ago extensive eruptions of this sort in the high central Sierra Nevada of California began to build up a blanket of rhyolitic ash flows several hundred feet thick over the western slopes, filling the valleys of westward-flowing streams. Later, the composition of the ash became andesitic and, with quantities of water, formed great *mudflows* that swept down the western canyons and out onto the margins of the Great Valley of California about 8 to 10 million years ago. On the east side of the Sierra Nevada the pinkish white Bishop Tuff was formed from ash flows about 700,000 years ago. *Tuff* is the name given to the rock formed from finer-grained pyroclastics. The Bishop Tuff is interbedded with glacial sediments on the eastern slopes of the Sierra. As in many such ash flows, the hot, viscous, glass particles became welded together to form solid rock. *Breccia* is a rock made up of large, angular fragments which are usually embedded in finer ash.

Great ash-flow sheets form the surface of the Pajorito Plateau near Alamos, New Mexico, and ash-flow sheets and alternating lava flows in the San Juan Mountains in Colorado cover 1,000 square miles with a volume of ash of over 1,000 cubic miles.

An example of a modern ash-flow sheet was built in the Valley of Ten Thousand Smokes in 1912 near Mount Katmai, Alaska. It is over 500 feet thick and its lower layers are welded.

On an early morning in 1902, Mount Pelée, in the West Indies, after being considered extinct, abruptly staged a series of four violent eruptions of glowing clouds of incandescent particles of dust and ash, mixed with hot, poisonous gases. Heavier than air, an ash flow called a *nuée ardente*, or *glowing cloud*, swept down like an avalanche across St. Pierre, setting it on fire and utterly destroying that city of 30,000 people. The story is persistent that only two men survived. One, a prisoner in an underground dungeon, survived to no real purpose, for, as soon as he recovered, he was executed for the crimes for which he had been imprisoned!

SUMMARY
A great deal is crammed into Chapter 4, but we do need to know something about the *processes* of volcanism, the *forms* that volcanic action constructs

(cinder cones, composite cones, lava cones, shield volcanoes, volcanic domes, volcanic plateaus, and others), and the *products* of volcanic activity. Without such basic knowledge we cannot get very far in the study of volcanoes!

There is no better way to study volcanoes than to observe, investigate, construct explanations, and test our theories in other situations. This is why we use so many examples. Among the world's greatest laboratories on volcanism have been Hawaii, Iceland, and the Mediterranean area.

Volcanoes erupt gases, molten lava, and rock. What is the most abundant gas erupted? Why do you think this is true? Is the rock erupted by volcanoes always volcanic rock? Description of a rock involves its mineral composition, chemical composition, texture, structure, and color. But description is just the beginning. We want to know also about a rock's origin: where did the rock come from and how did it form?

How do calderas form and grow? Can craters form without volcanic action? Why do we say that the earth is essentially a mass of igneous rock? Why the difference between aa and pahoehoe? Why do some volcanic rocks form columns, like the Devil's Postpile? Why is most volcanic glass rhyolitic in composition rather than basaltic? From what depth does magma come? How do we know? Why is andesite so much more abundant than rhyolite?

FIVE

HAWAIIAN AND FLOOD-BASALT ERUPTIONS:
THE SHIELD VOLCANOES AND FISSURE ERUPTIONS

PACIFIC HOTSPOT: THE HAWAIIAN VOLCANOES
Perched on the rim of Kilauea Caldera, 500 feet above a black lava lake, is the Hawaiian Volcano Observatory of the U.S. Geological Survey. Below is the 1,000-foot-wide Halemaumau Fire Pit, where dwelt Pele, the legendary goddess of fire.

Halemaumau is the active pit on the floor of Kilauea Caldera (Figure 5-1). About 2 miles across the caldera from the Observatory, and also on its rim, is the headquarters of Hawaii National Park. A mile or so from Park head-quarters is the pit crater of Kilauea Iki (Little Kilauea), active in 1959. Here, on Hawaii—the "Big Island"—is the world's greatest natural laboratory for the study of volcanoes and volcanism.

The Hawaiian Islands form a west-northwest trending chain of volcanic islands, in the subtropical latitudes of the mid-Pacific Ocean, extending for over 1,000 kilometers from Hawaii to Midway. The submarine chain, of which the Hawaiian Islands are the visible peaks, is at least twice as long.

The islands appear to lie along a great rift zone or fault in the Pacific Basin which has allowed basaltic lava to erupt in enormous volumes for at least the last 5 million years. Hawaii, at the southeast end of the chain, is the only island on which there are active volcanoes. Strangely, progressing toward the northwest, the volcanic islands and their rocks become older and older, like this: Hawaii, active from the present back to less than 1 million

Figure 5-1 Summit caldera of Kilauea Volcano. The caldera is floored by lava flows erupted in this century. The step faults by which the caldera is enlarged may be seen along the western and northern margins. The "Firepit" Halemaumau, a pit crater about 500 feet deep in this 1954 photo, is near the southwest edge of the caldera. Halemaumau is the present area of activity. The volcano observatory of the U.S. Geological Survey is on the northwest rim of Kilauea. (*Aerial oblique photo by the U.S. Geological Survey, looking in a northerly direction.*)

years ago, Maui and Molokai 0.8 to 1.8 million years ago, Oahu (on which Honolulu is located) about 2.2 to 2.5 million years ago, and Kauai 3.8 to 5.6 million years ago. *Why*?

The concept of plate tectonics offers a suggestion. Perhaps the huge Pacific Plate is moving northwestward across a hot spot of magma which is presently under the island of Hawaii. Thus, in 5 million years the island of Kauai has moved on past the hot spot about 500 miles! Very roughly, this is 6 inches a year—not out of line with plate tectonics theory.

The 4,000 square mile island of Hawaii is built up of thousands and thousands of flows, and intermittent ash falls, of black basaltic lava—the biggest pile of geologically young volcanic material on earth! From the depth of the ocean at about 18,000 feet to the top of the volcano Mauna Loa at 13,680 feet is about 6 miles. That's higher than Mount Everest! The mountain's volume is approximately 50,000 cubic kilometers, and the part above sea level is about 60 miles long by half as wide. Mauna Loa is a typical *dome* or *shield volcano*. At its crest is a huge caldera, 600 feet deep, over 9,000 feet wide, and nearly 20,000 feet in its longest dimension. Lava periodically pours from fissures on the floor of the caldera and the flanks of the dome. Weak explosions sometimes occur, and there are small volcanic cones on the caldera floor.

Kilauea Caldera is about 30 miles down the east flank of the dome of Mauna Loa at elevation 4,000 feet. Every few years, the lava lake in Halemaumau rises and lava fountains high into the air. But most often, the lava breaks out along fissures in one of the great rift zones that cut across the slopes of Mauna Loa and Kilauea. In relation to Kilauea, these are principally the Southwest rift zone, the Northeast rift zone, and the East rift zone. Typically, lava eruptions break out somewhere along fissures in a rift zone and then centralize and develop a new pit crater. In recent years, several pit craters have developed in this way along the East rift zone: Aloi Crater (230 feet deep) in 1962, Makaopuhi (740 feet deep), active in 1965, and then a new one, Mauna Ulu, in 1969. On a day in that year I was fortunate enough to stand on the crater rim of Mauna Ulu and watch the spectacular fountaining, up to hundreds of feet in the air, and the cascading of fire-red molten lava. No other geological phenomenon ever so greatly impressed me, unless, perhaps, it was the 20-foot-high fault scarp at Hebgen Lake in 1959! Mauna Ulu became quiet and the lava lake crusted over in 1971; but only temporarily; at this writing (1974) eruption has been resumed.

By the year 1790, the long history of quiet eruptions of lava on Hawaii had lulled native Hawaiians into a feeling of safety and security. But that year a company of Keoua's army, marching across the desert on the lee side of Kilauea after battles with Kamehameha, was killed by violent explosive eruptions originating northeast of Halemaumau pit. The warriors had stopped near Keanakakoi Crater to make offerings to propitiate Pele, so the hapless Hawaiians probably wondered at the sudden anger of their goddess of fire! At any rate, Keoua broke up his army (which included women, children, and pigs) into three divisions. The first division got through without losses, but the third division, which had followed the second by 2 hours, found all of that group dead from poison gas. Footprints of the stricken people are still preserved in the ash along this old trail.

Volcanologists think that, in the violent eruptions of 1790 and in similar eruptions, an influx of ground water reached hot lava and caused the unusual explosions.

Five great volcanoes make up the island of Hawaii, but three are extinct. One of these—Mauna Kea—is 13,784 feet in elevation and shows evidence of glaciation within the last several thousand years. Mauna Kea is the highest island peak on earth. It is a basaltic shield volcano but its most recent activity brought andesitic materials to cap the mountain. Flying over the mountain at very low altitude in 1969, I saw no prominent crater, but the summit area was covered with a number of small, reddish cinder cones, developed in the last andesitic stage of eruption.

One of the most frequently seen and photographed volcanoes in the world is Diamond Head, at the entrance of Honolulu harbor and directly in the path of low-flying aircraft coming and going to Honolulu and Pearl Harbor. Visitors can drive into the flat-floored crater. The volcano consists principally of tuff and breccia formed by explosions about 2 million years ago when hot lavas encountered sea water. Diamond Head stands as a world-renowned symbol of the state of Hawaii.

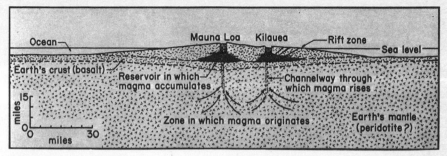

Figure 5-2 An inferred cross section through Mauna Loa and Kilauea, Hawaii. (*U.S. Geological Survey.*)

Where does the magma come from that feeds Mauna Loa and Kilauea, the two active volcanic centers on the island of Hawaii (Figure 5-2)?

Research at the Volcano Observatory shows that basaltic magma originates about 60 kilometers deep, in the low-velocity zone in the upper mantle where melting takes place to form magma chambers. From there the magma rises through pipes and fractures to smaller, local reservoirs 1 or 2 kilometers from the surface shortly before eruptions occur. Doming of the land surface above the shallow magma reservoirs and a rise in lava lakes like Halemaumau take place before eruption. During this process, cooling, partial crystallization, and crystal settling tend to divide the magmas into fractions with differing composition. Thus, the composition of Hawaiian lava eruptions differs from time to time and place to place.

COLUMBIA RIVER PLATEAU

In the Snake River Canyon and along the upper part of the Columbia River, deeply eroded canyons expose thousands of layers of flat-lying basalt flows—*flood basalts*. These were formed in middle to late Miocene time between 18 and 10 million years ago by eruptions of highly fluid lava which spread for miles from long fissures, filling lakes and canyons and covering the land surface to an average depth of about 1,800 feet. The area once covered was about 150,000 square miles, and some individual flows have been traced for 150 kilometers. Erosion has removed much of the original basalt but large plateau areas remain in northeastern Oregon, southeastern Washington, and adjacent parts of Idaho. Many of the basalt flows developed vertical joints as they cooled. There is evidence that the earth's crust sagged under the enormous load of lava.

LAVA BEDS NATIONAL MONUMENT AND THE MODOC PLATEAU

South of the Columbia Plateau, fissure eruptions of basalt continued in southeastern Oregon, northeastern California, and northwestern Nevada. Much flood basalt was erupted in these areas from Miocene, through Pliocene, and into Holocene time. The great chain of Cascade volcanoes extends from north to south along the full length of the western boundary of the Miocene-to-Holocene flood basalt province.

An area of about 13,000 square miles of the plateau in northeastern California is called the Modoc Plateau. It includes a great variety of lava flows, ash, volcanic breccias, mudflows, and volcanic domes, ranging from basalt to rhyolitic obsidian. The area is an irregular, stream-dissected, mountainous plateau averaging about 4,500 feet above sea level.

In the western part of the Modoc Plateau an area of about 80 square miles has been set aside as Lava Beds National Monument. Geologically, it consists wholly of the Holocene Modoc basalt, featured by a succession of pahoehoe flows containing over 300 lava tubes ranging from a few feet to 75 feet in diameter. Some have several levels and many have collapsed to form winding trenches miles long. Lava columns have built up from their floors and lava stalactites hang from their roofs. Pressure domes appear on the surface and lava spurting out of the tubes here and there has made spectacular *spatter cones* a few feet high.

It is in this fantastic country that the Modoc Indians established their hiding places during the Modoc War of 1872–1873. The extreme complexities of the intricate passageways enabled Captain Jack and his Indians to frustrate the United States Army for almost two years!

SUMMARY

In terms of sheer bulk, Mauna Loa and the other volcanoes of the Island of Hawaii are the greatest on earth. Mauna Loa and Mauna Kea tower more than 30,000 feet above the sea floor. They are the greatest of the world's shield volcanoes. They are also the world's most intensively studied volcanoes, largely because of the Volcano Observatory of the U.S. Geological Survey, on the rim of Kilauea, and the University of Hawaii in Honolulu.

Probably 99.99 percent of the rock of the Hawaiian Islands is basalt. Why? Still, a small fraction is rhyolite. How could the rhyolite have formed? Where are there other basaltic shield volcanoes in the world?

The Hawaiian volcanoes are located in the mid-Pacific but apparently not on a midoceanic ridge. How do volcanologists account for their location, the elongate trend of the islands, and the regular progression in ages of their volcanoes, from northwest to southeast?

The Columbia River Plateau and the Modoc Plateau represent tremendous outpourings of basaltic lava, plus intermittent local explosive activity, during the last 18 million years. Can you tie this into plate tectonics theory?

SIX

ERUPTIVE VIOLENCE: SOME TYPE VOLCANOES AND ERUPTIONS

ICELAND, ON THE MID-ATLANTIC RIDGE

In the cold, black darkness of the early morning of January 23, 1973, a glowing red-orange curtain of fire shot from a new mile-long fissure on the west slope of Helgafell, an "extinct" volcano (Kirkjufell, Figures 6-1 and 6-2) on the island of Heimaey off the coast of southern Iceland. Great billowing clouds of steam and ash—white by day and black by night—soon extended as high as 30,000 feet above the fountains of orange-hot lava. The blackness of the dark clouds of steam, ash, and cinders was relieved by frequent flashes of internal lightning and by the red fire below. Tremendous explosive sounds added to the awesome view.

With remarkable efficiency and discipline—advised by United Nations disaster consultant Will H. Perry, a Californian—all 5,500 people of the fishing village of Vestmannaeyjar were safely evacuated to Reykjavik by 9 P.M. on the same day! The few officials and scientists who remained behind—equipped with headgear and gas masks—saw lava bombs hurtling through the air, falling ash choking their streets and loading the roofs of their homes, and lava flowing from the widening fissures less than 1 mile from town.

By the end of the second day, the long fissure which had developed on the 23rd was closing, and cratering had begun. Fountaining of lava along the fissure was gradually being cut off and activity had concentrated on the building of a combined cinder-and-spatter cone made up of hardened lava fragments and congealed blobs or spatters. The new cone—named

Figure 6-1 Sheets of orange-red fiery lava and incandescent volcanic ash erupting from the flanks of the new volcano, Kirkjufell, on the island of Heimaey, January 1973. Note the mile-long fissure eruptions at the near-base of the volcanic cone. (*Will H. Perry, Jr., photo.*)

Kirkjufell—soon grew to a height of 700 feet. Much ash continued to fall and black, Hawaiian-type, basaltic lava was being produced at 100 cubic meters per second.

By January 26, the ash fall had become so heavy that roofs were collapsing and ash accumulations in the city had reached a depth of one meter. Bombs continued to fall, and new eruptions in the sea began to peril the valuable fishing harbor. By the 31st it was estimated that 2 million cubic meters of ash had fallen on Vestmannaeyjar and 120 buildings had collapsed. Ash production and lava flows had continued to increase; lava was flowing at up to 15 meters per hour.

Large volumes of gas were erupted with the ash. Apart from water, the principal gases were carbon dioxide (98 percent), carbon monoxide, and methane. The only person killed in the entire series of eruptions on Heimaey was a man who entered a cellar without a gas mask.

By February 20, the western wall of Kirkjufell had collapsed under the pressure of lava. Finally, lava flows became the dominant type of eruption. Flows up to 100 meters thick began to engulf houses on the edge of town and to spread into the sea, threatening to fill the harbor.

In a few months, lava beneath the sea at Heimaey had accumulated to 65 million cubic meters and on the land to 36 million cubic meters. An estimated

23 million cubic meters of tephra had been deposited and the total of all materials produced by Kirkjufell was over 130 million cubic meters.

Their harbor and their remaining homes threatened by advancing lava, the Icelanders began a remarkable experiment. They flooded hot, slowly moving lava flows with large quantities of cold sea water, slowly cooling the flows enough so that their fishing harbor remained useful and half their homes habitable.

Before activity died down in June, 300 buildings had been destroyed by fire and lava and another 70 had been buried by tephra. Kirkjufell had added a half square mile to the 8 square mile island of Heimaey—itself built from the sea by the volcano Helgafell about 5,000 to 6,000 years ago.

The action at Heimaey in 1973 and the building of the new, neighboring island of Surtsey by similar volcanic processes in 1963 are spectacular expressions of the consequences of Iceland's position astride the spreading Mid-Atlantic Ridge. Along its central rift, the crust of the Atlantic Ocean is splitting apart, flood basalts are emerging, and—according to the theory of plate tectonics—the North American and Eurasian crustal plates are drifting apart.

In 1783, the people of southern Iceland witnessed the only known historic eruption of flood basalts. From the spreading rifts across Iceland—

Figure 6-2 Glowing curtain of lava and hot ash with a dark cloud of steam and volcanic dust erupt from Kirkjufell on the island of Heimaey. The white cross and arch are the gate of a cemetery which has been buried by black tephra. (*Will H. Perry, Jr., photo.*)

marked by faults and a central *graben*, or trough—there issued about 2.8 cubic miles of lava. Lava spread from a fissure 32 kilometers long to cover an area of 560 square kilometers. Twenty percent of Iceland's 50,000 people were killed. Only prehistoric plateau basalts—like those of the Miocene Columbia River Plateau, where individual flood-basalt lava flows of as much as 600 cubic miles have been measured—approach this 1783 Laki eruption in volume of lava. The largest historic Hawaiian flows have erupted up to 0.11 cubic miles of basaltic lava.

ERUPTIVE TYPES

No two volcanoes are alike and no two have had precisely the same history. Yet we can classify them into a few broad groups based on (1) characteristic landforms (Chapter 1), (2) kinds of materials erupted (Chapter 4), and (3) types of volcanic activity. These three features, of course, are interdependent; one is dependent upon the other. For instance, in the *Hawaiian* type of eruptive activity (Chapter 5), the relatively quiet eruption of fluid, basaltic lavas builds up low shield volcanoes, and the vast eruptions of flood basalts build lava plateaus. Thus, the landforms are the result of the kinds of material erupted and the type of volcanic activity.

Contrasted with the Hawaiian eruptive type is the predominantly *explosive* eruptive type. We have seen that the more viscous, higher-silica magma favors explosive eruption and that the typical landform developed is the volcanic cone. Many variations occur. *Vulcanian* explosive activity, for example, involves viscous magma and moderate-to-strong explosions—like the activity of Vulcano near Italy—with short, stubby lava flows; beautiful cones are built. *Strombolian* explosive activity—like that of Stromboli, Italy—erupts moderately fluid lava, often in lava fountains, with many bombs and much tephra to form cinder cones. The term *Pelean eruption* is used for explosive action where domes or spines are developed—as in Mount Pelée on the island of Martinique in the West Indies—and glowing clouds are characteristic. Lassen Peak in northern California is a dacite plug dome. Extremely violent eruptive activity—like that described at Vesuvius by Pliny the Elder—has sometimes been called the *Plinian* eruptive type. Pliny the Elder, commanding the Roman fleet in the year 79 A.D. at the time of the violent eruptions which formed the modern Mt. Vesuvius and destroyed the cities of Pompeii and Herculaneum, got too close to the action and lost his life by suffocation by "sulphurous vapors." Pliny the Younger—the nephew of Pliny the Elder—left the account for posterity. In Plinian eruptions, great violence like that of Krakatoa in the East Indies and of perhistoric Mount Mazama (Crater Lake, Oregon) may leave great calderas without building a cone. Enormous volumes of tephra are erupted.

The type of volcanic activity and kind of material extruded usually vary from time to time in the history of a volcano. We know of no volcano, whose historical record is long, which has not exhibited more than one type of eruptive activity. Not uncommonly, three different types of activity take place during the history of a single volcano.

COMPOSITE VOLCANOES

The most famous, the most spectacular, and the most beautiful volcanoes in the world are the composite volcanoes, also called *stratovolcanoes* because they are made up of layers of ash, cinder, and lava. Most of the world's large, active volcanoes are composite.

The most ideally symmetrical large cone is 8,000-foot Mayon Volcano on Luzon Island in the Philippines. Its beautiful symmetry, with slopes rising on steepening concave curves, is the result of a small, constant central vent from which tephra and lava are erupted from time to time. Mayon is noted for mudflows which buried the town of Cagsaua at the base of the volcano in 1814, much as Herculaneum was buried at the foot of Vesuvius in 79 A.D.

Cascade Range The Cascade Range—including dozens of volcanoes, mostly composite—extends almost due north from Lassen Peak in northern California to Mount Baker in Washington. At least 15 of the largest should be considered recent and of these, 7—Lassen Peak, Cinder Cone, Mount Shasta, Mount Hood, Mount St. Helens, Mount Rainier, and Mount Baker—have erupted within the last two centuries. All have beautiful cones, and all have erupted tephra in great quantities; andesitic to rhyolitic lava and mudflows have moved down the flanks of all. Apart from such generalizations, each has had its own unique history.

Lassen Peak (Figure 2-1) Lassen is a steep, rough cone, 10,453 feet in elevation, set in the midst of the 170 square mile Lassen Volcanic National Park. The Park is a marvelous volcanic laboratory, for it exhibits composite volcanoes of several types, cinder cones, lava flows, lava tubes, hot springs, and fumaroles ("smoke holes").

Volcanic activity in Lassen Park began in Pliocene time with a series of basalt flows, followed by highly fluid flows of pyroxene andesite. These lie in a basin on top of the Mesozoic and older granitic and metamorphic rocks of the Sierra Nevada. During buildup of the plateau lavas, streams of fluid dacite erupted in Pleistocene time to form the black, glassy, columnar lavas that now encircle the peak. This was followed by more viscous, gas-poor dacite which welled up sluggishly in Lassen's vent to fill the crater; thus Lassen Peak is a "plug dome." A number of lesser dacite domes nearby, called Chaos Crags, erupted ash and pumice about 200 years ago; plugs of viscous dacite were pushed up to build the domes. The Cinder Cone is a classically beautiful, symmetrical, dark cone which was formed by eruptions of tephra about 500 years ago.

Lassen Peak burst into explosive eruption in 1914, and a year later lava rose in the small summit crater and spilled over its rim. The molten lava initiated extensive mudflows as it hit snow high on the mountain's slopes. A major blast from the side of the crater on May 22, 1915, caused a glowing cloud to sweep down the northeast slope, burning all trees to form what is now called the *Devastated Area*. Activity ceased in 1917, but hot springs, fumaroles, and mud volcanoes are numerous today. The springs erupt sulfuric acid, hydrogen sulfide, sulfur, silica, water, clay, and mud.

Figure 6-3 The vent of *Mount Erebus*, rising from sea level to 12,447 feet over a distance of 10 miles, located on Ross Island at latitude 77°S off Victoria Land, Antarctica. The island was first sighted by Sir James Clark Ross in 1841 during his 1839–1943 Antarctic Expedition. Though Ross's ships *Terror* and *Erebus* landed on Possession Island and others in clear sight of the continent, it was not until 1895 that the first party landed on the continent at Cape Adare. This active volcano is characterized by Strombolian-type eruptions. The rock is the rather unusual low-silica anorthoclase phonolite. (*U.S. Navy photo. Submitted by Wulf Massel, Indiana University, courtesy of National Association of Geology teachers, Journal of Geological Education, May 1973.*)

Mount Shasta The double-peaked composite volcano, Mount Shasta (Figure 4-1), about 80 miles north of Lassen, is at an elevation of 14,162 feet—about 10,000 feet above its base. The volcano has a volume of 80 cubic miles of tephra and lava!

Bedrock under this vast pile of volcanics consists of Cretaceous and older sedimentary and metamorphic rocks of the eastern Klamath Mountains. Altered Miocene volcanics lie on the older rocks and are, in turn, overlain by Pliocene andesite flows. The great cone of Shasta was built entirely within Quaternary time. The earliest Pleistocene lavas were basaltic andesite; later lavas were pyroxene andesite and dacite, with interbedded tephra.

Late in its history, a new vent high on the slopes of Shasta formed the satellitic cone called Shastina on an east-west fissure. During the latest ice age, small alpine glaciers extended down the slopes of the mountain. Some of the eruptions of Shastina were postglacial, but the latest eruptions of Shasta have come from the summit crater, now about 600 feet across. The materials erupted included pumice, cinders, lapilli, blocks, and volcanic bombs. It is likely that the latest of such eruptions was the pumice eruption in 1786; at least, the explorer, La Perouse, made such an observation while cruising along the California coast during that year.

Mount Erebus Mount Erebus (Figure 6-3), an active, composite cone, rises 13,200 feet on Ross Island in Antarctica. Sir James Ross sighted the volcano, which was "emitting smoke and flame," in 1841 from his ship *Erebus*.

Erebus, the most active volcano in Antarctica, is one of four which have built up Ross Island. The volcano—visited occasionally during the present century, and in 1972–1973 by a New Zealand Antarctic Research team— shows a constant plume of steam and is occasionally lit up by outbursts of ash and lava bombs. A molten lake of lava lies on the crater floor about 150 meters below the summit rim.

The rock type is rather unusual, consisting of large crystals of anorthoclase, a sodium potassium feldspar, embedded in a glassy groundmass containing tiny crystals of olivine, pyroxene, and nepheline (a sodium potassium silicate). Studies of magnetic polarity show that the main volcanic cone has been built within the last 700,000 years.

The 1973 team of geologists witnessed 35 small, explosive eruptions within 2 weeks. Fresh volcanic bombs around the crater are up to 1 meter or more in length. An unusual note: Erebus is known for its ejected crystals of anorthoclase, and also for its 60-foot towers of ice formed from the action of water-rich fumaroles.

Cerro Negro Cerro Negro (Figure 6-4), elevation 1,615 feet, is a very active, highly explosive composite volcano in Nicaragua, a country of many active volcanoes. Its eruptions are characteristically of the Strombolian type— moderately fluid basalt, short flows, ejection of many pasty blobs and bombs—erupting great clouds of ash, cinders, bombs, and steam. Mudflows frequently move down Cerro Negro's steep slopes.

The photo shows the 1971 eruption, with features of the cinder cone and elements of the eruption.

CINDER CONES

By definition, cinder cones are volcanic peaks built entirely of cinders and other volcanic fragments; more properly they should be called *tephra* cones. Ideally, they are truncated cones circular in plan, with steep, symmetrical slopes and bowl-shaped craters which are quite large compared with their heights. Most are andesitic or basaltic in composition. They are formed by explosive ejection of solid fragments of volcanic rock, by glassy fragments made of volcanic rock, or by glassy fragments made by frothing of lava rising in a vent and crater. Their type of eruption might be called *Strombolian*. Their form is due to the fact that the largest and densest fragments fall closest to the vent. The angle of slope depends on the angle at which the fragments can remain at rest, usually about 20 to 30°. If blobs of liquid lava are thrown out, a steeper-sided, irregular spatter cone is formed.

Figure 6-4 Eruption of Cerro Negro, an active composite volcano in Nicaragua, in 1971. A symmetrical cinder cone has been built up by the most recent phase of the volcano's activity, but lava flows at its base (left middle ground and foreground) attest to fluid eruptions, also. The dense cloud erupting from the crater is dark and heavy with pyroclastic fragments (tephra) near the crater; then, as most of the fragments are deposited, the white cloud downwind consists mostly of steam. Older volcanoes, now covered with vegetation, may be seen in the upper left and background. (*Courtesy of California Division of Mines and Geology, Bulletin 198, 1973.*)

Cinder cones are small volcanoes, rarely over 1,200 feet high. The reinforcement of layers of lava appears to be necessary to build up the huge composite volcanoes. Cinder cones are often satellitic or secondary. That is, they develop on the flanks, at the bases, or within the craters of greater volcanoes, or along rifts in Hawaiian-type eruptions. The many little cinder cones in the great erosional caldera of 10,000-foot Haleakala on Maui and on the summit of 13,784-foot Mauna Kea on Hawaii are late phases of volcanism caused perhaps by increased viscosity of the magma, but increased gas content might also be a factor in the change to explosive activity.

Many things can happen to break the symmetry of cinder cones. They may be multiple or overlapping, as along a rift zone. Borne by the winds, ash and cinders will build up a higher rim downwind. Diamond Head, the renowned landmark of Honolulu, is a large cinder cone formed by explosions when hot magma encountered sea water. Its crater is a bowl about 400 feet deep and 5,000 feet across, with the southwestern rim at elevation 775 feet and the northeastern rim rising to 460 feet. Cinder cones may also have their symmetry upset by successive explosions on their flanks or at their bases, instead of vertically upward from a single vent. But most often the form of a cinder cone is altered by eruptions of lava, breaching the crater walls if from the central vent, or perhaps breaking out on the flanks or at the base of the cone.

Amboy Crater   Surrounded by 24 square miles of recent black lava flows, Amboy (Figure 6-5) is a small cinder cone—one of many—in the heart of the Mojave Desert in southeastern California. The peak has a profile like a cone which has been truncated close to its base. It is about 1,500 feet across at its base but only 250 feet high.

Exploring this area some years ago, I was most impressed by the large number of hummocky, disrupted flows of olivine basalt and low, oval lava "blisters" a few feet high—often split down their length and hollow inside. Heaps of basalt blocks, volcanic bombs, small bowl-shaped explosion

Figure 6-5   Amboy Crater, Mojave Desert, California. This is a beautiful example of the typical cinder cone, only a few hundred feet high with an extremely large crater in proportion to its height. During one of its latest eruptions the cone was breached and lava flowed out over the geologically young desert-like sediments. There is no specific historic record of its last eruption, but it was probably only a few hundred years ago. Note the black lava flows in the upper right corner. (*Drawn by Peter H. Oakeshott from photos.*)

Figure 6-6   Paricutin Volcano in eruption in mid-1944 about 1¹/₂ years after it began to form. Here the near-perfect cinder cone has reached a height above its base of over 1,000 feet. (*Drawn by Peter H. Oakeshott from photos.*)

depressions, and collapsed pahoehoe lava ridges made the walk to the crater a rough one!

Amboy Crater is really a closely coalescing group of cones built up by at least six periods of eruption. Its latest phase was the breaching of the crater by a basalt flow which extended out across the Late Quaternary sediments of desert Bristol Lake. Amboy erupted about 6,000 years ago, according to radiocarbon dates.

Paricutin Volcano   No cinder cone is better known scientifically or is more instructive than Paricutin Volcano (Figure 6-6), Mexico, for it was born in 1943 and has grown to maturity—if not old age—under our eyes.

On February 20 of that year a farmer was startled to see a small crack in the ground in his cornfield open up and begin to emit hot sulfurous fumes. In a few minutes he began to feel earthquakes, and ash, steam, and rock fragments were erupted around him. By the next day a new cinder cone had been built 25 feet high, reaching 400 feet within a week, and a month later a beautiful, black, symmetrical, truncated cone had been built 1,000 feet above the Mexican plateau—itself nearly 10,000 feet in elevation.

Ejected from Paricutin were glassy ash in great quantities, cinders, lapilli, and bombs. Shortly, lava began to flow from the base and flanks of the cone, spreading out for several miles and engulfing two small towns. Water content of the erupted products was measured at about 1 percent by weight. Hottest temperature of the molten basalt was 1135°C; lowest in the moving flows was 750°C.

Paricutin's activity lasted until 1952, but materials erupted in the last few years slid down the 30° slopes and maintained the height of the crater rim at about 1,000 feet. The eruptive history of Paricutin was typically Strombolian—moderate eruptions, interspersed occasionally with violent eruptions, with more-or-less continuous activity over a period of years. The ejecta—erupted materials—were also characteristic of Strombolian eruptions.

SUMMARY

No two volcanoes are alike in their eruptive history, yet we must classify in order to appreciate and gain understanding of characteristic volcanic activity. An obvious basis for classification is the form of the volcano—shield volcanoes and cinder cones, for example. Certainly a second obvious grouping is the kind of material erupted; the rhyolite domes are very different, for example, from the basaltic shield volcanoes. Third, the kind of eruptive activity—quiet lava flow, violent explosive activity, characteristic glowing cloud eruptions—is a basis for discussion of volcanoes. See Figures 6-7 and 6-8.

We have discussed specific examples within each of these groups, and, in so doing, have learned something of the world's great volcanoes. We

Figure 6-7 Idealized internal structure of a cinder cone. Note the various layers of tephra of different coarseness which have built up a symmetrical cone, the breccia-filled pipe or vent spilling out into the relatively large crater, and the black pipe and dike of lava. (*Scratchboard drawing by Peter H. Oakeshott, from various sources.*)

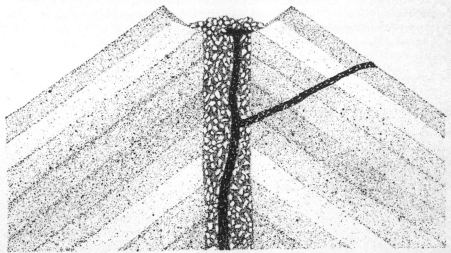

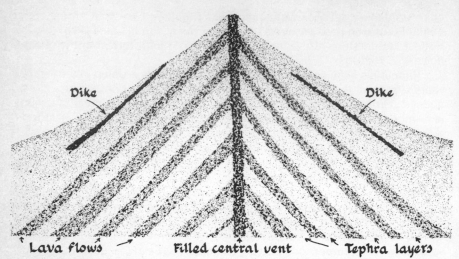

Dike

Dike

Lava flows → Filled central vent ← Tephra layers

Figure 6-8 Idealized internal structure of a composite volcano. Layers of dark andesitic lava alternate with layers of tephra or fragmental material. Occasional black, sheetlike layers of lava cut across the structure as dikes. Lava in the central vent may well up to fill the small crater to form the plug-dome volcano, like Lassen Peak. (*Scratchboard drawing by Peter H. Oakeshott, from various sources.*)

cannot discuss volcanoes without learning something of the classic Hawaiian shield volcanoes, the great composite cones and plug domes of the Cascade Range, and sea-floor spreading on the Mid-Atlantic Ridge in Iceland. Wherever we can see activity today we can increase our understanding of volcanism of past ages.

If you are interested in volcanoes, expand your knowledge by looking up others in the literature. For each: Why do you think it has the external form it has developed? Why does it erupt basalt or rhyolite, or andesitic ash, or whatever it does erupt? Why has its history been largely explosive, or quiet eruption, or varied from time to time? Of course, you won't find all the answers, but you'll learn a lot about volcanoes while looking and trying!

SEVEN

LATE STAGES OF VOLCANISM AND VOLCANIC AFTERMATH

FUMAROLES, HOT SPRINGS, AND GEYSERS

All through the life of a volcanic eruption—of any type—gases and water are emitted. Some volcanoes even start with eruption of steam and sulfurous gases. The most persistent of all products of volcanism is water. As the heat of volcanic eruption is reduced and a volcano becomes dormant and finally extinct, the flow of lava ceases and explosive eruption of tephra comes to an end. Gases amount to less than 1 percent by weight of an active eruption, but when eruption of lava and/or tephra ceases, the volcanic gases—including water—become the sole product.

Fumaroles—originally from a Latin word meaning *to smoke*—are vents other than a central volcanic vent or crater, from which gases and water are erupted. A *hot spring* is a quiet, nonexplosive discharge of hot or warm water. *Geysers* are eruptive hot springs. *Solfataras* are fumaroles in which sulfurous gases—like hydrogen sulfide (H_2S), sulfur dioxide (SO_2), and sulfur (S)—are important. The word comes from Solfatara Volcano, Italy.

What are the constituents of the eruptions of fumaroles and geysers? They are precisely the same as the gaseous emanations of volcanic eruptions (Chapter 4), namely: about 99 percent water, followed in lessening amounts by carbon dioxide, sulfurous gases, methane (CH_4), ammonia (NH_3), hydrochloric acid (HCl), hydrofluoric acid (HF), and hydrogen (H_2) gas. Traces of metallic elements—such as iron, copper, mercury, lead, tungsten, manganese, and zinc—are common; but some hot springs deposit concentrated metallic compounds. Some of the hot-water wells in the Salton Sea area are unusually high in silver and copper. Radon—a radioactive gas—is found in some hot springs. As we have seen (Chapter 4), most of these gases are highly active in the presence of hot water and combine chemically with the constituents of rocks in and around the vents. Production of steam for energy in the Salton Sea area will probably be accompanied by commerical production of chlorides of Na, Ca, and K.

Not all fumaroles erupt all these materials in the same proportions, but one or the other may be dominant. Elemental sulfur near volcanic vents was so abundant at Mount Etna and some of the other Italian volcanoes that it was of commerical importance before the refining of petroleum became the world's greatest source of sulfur. Years ago (1933–1954) large quantities of carbon dioxide for making dry ice were produced from wells drilled into hot spring areas in the Salton Sea basin in southeastern California. But one of the major problems of the operation was the buildup of calcium carbonate $(CaCO_3)$ deposits, thus sealing well perforations and reducing the diameter of conduits. Some fumaroles are very high in methane, a combustible gas. It must be understood, of course, that each of these substances may originate in ways other than by volcanism; much methane, for example, forms from the decay of organic matter.

The colors of the waters and rocks in and around hot springs and geysers—particularly the reds, yellows, and browns—are mostly the results of the formation of iron compounds by chemical reaction of rocks, water, and acidic or alkaline solutions. One of the commonest alteration products is clay, formed by hot-water alteration of volcanic ash or tuff. Colored mud and clay often form "paint pots," as in Yellowstone National Park and at Bumpass' Hell in Lassen Volcanic National Park. Erupted mud may build up mud "volcanoes" a few inches to a few feet high. Other colors in hot-spring areas are due to the algae which live in waters of different temperatures.

The gases and water of fumaroles may come from deep-seated magma bodies and/or from groundwater which originated at the earth's surface. Perhaps most often the hot water is groundwater that has penetrated cracks and fractures to come into contact with hot volcanic rock or magma. Magma, at depth, cools very slowly. In the huge, deep-seated bodies of magma which cool and solidify at depths of several miles to form granite *batholiths* in the cores of mountain ranges, it is known that cooling to form solid rock may require a million years or more! Smaller bodies of magma may supply heat for many thousands of years.

Hot waters dissolve all manner of substances, but among the commonest are calcium carbonate $(CaCO_3)$ and silica (SiO_2). As hot water brings such substances to the surface, pressure and temperature are reduced, evaporation takes place, and cones, domes, terraces, and irregular shapes are built up.

Yellowstone National Park A wonderland of geysers, hot springs, and fumaroles of all types and forms has been set aside in the northwestern corner of Wyoming and adjacent borders of Montana. The area is part of the

Yellowstone Plateau in the Rocky Mountains, which averages about 7,500 feet in elevation. The Yellowstone River, flowing northward and northeastward into the Missouri River, has cut more than 1,200 feet down into the Plateau, thereby exposing thick, nearly horizontal layers of rhyolite flows and several huge rhyolite ash-flow sheets.

Dr. Gordon A. Macdonald (a specialist on Hawaiian volcanism) and other geologists of the U.S. Geological Survey ascribe the enormous volume of rhyolite and the principal building of the Yellowstone Plateau to three separate cycles of eruption. The first, starting about 2 million years ago, left the largest caldera yet recognized on earth—at least 50 miles long—over the Yellowstone and Island Park area, 40 miles west of Yellowstone Lake. The youngest caldera—representing collapse after the third great cycle of eruption—formed about 600,000 years ago and was 30 to 50 miles across. It may still be seen on satellite imagery. Some geologists theorize that the enormous plateau of rhyolite represents the top of a granite batholith that approached the surface of the earth. The great volume of heat in the rhyolite mass and below heats up groundwater and furnishes the energy for the abundance of spectacular and colorful hot-spring features of the Park.

Yellowstone is known for its geysers more than any other feature; in fact, the U.S. Geological Survey notes that a large proportion of the geysers of the world are in Yellowstone Park (200). The name geyser, for an eruptive hot spring, came from the Great Geysir, one of 30 in Iceland. Others are found in Chile, New Zealand (22), and the Kamchatka Peninsula. The Beowawe area in central Nevada once had about 20 small geysers, which have lately quit erupting. Casa Diablo Hot Springs, Mono County, California, once had a geyser; my family and I saw it erupt about 40 years ago.

Among the beautiful geysers of Yellowstone which have been visited by so many millions of vacationers are Daisy Geyser (now dormant but it used to erupt at an angle, not vertically), Lone Star (which has built up a steep siliceous-sinter dome), Little Whirligig, Midway, Riverside, Seismic, Steamboat, and the world-renowned Old Faithful. Most geysers erupt at irregular intervals, but Old Faithful is on a more regular schedule. Still, I remember years ago waiting anywhere from 40 to 80 minutes for the deafening roar and blast of steam 100 feet or so into the air. As in many geysers, an inconspicuous premonitory overflow of water just precedes the main eruption. This action reduces pressure on the column of hot water below and causes it to flash into steam. Steamboat Geyser in Yellowstone may be the largest in the world; its eruptions have been as high as 300 feet.

Why do the great majority of hot springs bubble water quietly to the surface, while an occasional one is violently eruptive?

The most plausible theory goes like this: Below the land surface is an intricate plumbing system of fractures and irregular passageways into which groundwater seeps. A deeper heat source warms the water in the intricate passageways to boiling temperature. The deeper the water the higher the pressure and the higher the boiling point. Hot water is lighter than cold and so tends to rise. As heat accumulates and pressure is reduced by overflow at the vent, the whole column of water may flash into steam and rush out explosively.

The delicate balance in this process of geysering means that geysers may stop or start, or vary in their behavior quite readily. Passages may become blocked, water circulation may change, or water temperatures may change. The Hebgen Lake earthquake near West Yellowstone in 1959 started the eruptions of Seismic Geyser and many hot springs became eruptive; Sapphire Geyser greatly increased its activity. Other small geysers in Yellowstone ceased their activity. In terms of geologic time, a geyser is short-lived.

ENERGY FROM VOLCANIC HEAT

We have no idea how long ago mankind first used natural hot waters for bathing, cleaning, keeping warm, and even for cooking! The more sophisticated use of natural hot water for heating homes and greenhouses began commercially in Iceland in 1925 and continues quite successfully today. For generations, hot springs have been widely considered to have value in curing all manner of illnesses, and all over the world people have come to drink the mineral waters and to take hot-water and mud baths. Thus, areas of hot springs and geysers first became fashionable spas, then more permanent recreation centers, and finally many were built up as towns and cities.

The potential of natural hot water and steam for generation of electricity was recognized not long after man began to generate electricity as a major source of power, but in the early 1900s drilling techniques were not adequate and problems of corrosion of pipes and generators by acidic or strongly alkaline waters were extremely difficult.

The geologic conditions necessary for development of power from natural steam are quite special: (1) a constant, shallow, buried source of heat such as a body of magma or very hot igneous rock; (2) a large reservoir of highly porous rock, fractured or cavernous, with a source of sufficient groundwater under pressure to be heated to temperatures above the boiling point of water at the land surface, so that it flashes into "dry" steam as it emerges from the well; and (3) some kind of more-or-less impervious rock layers that reduce the natural loss of underground water and heat to the surface.

Of course, there must also be a market for the power not too far away. With all these factors—plus noise pollution and waste disposal—to consider, only four areas in the world now use geothermal power to generate considerable amounts of electrical energy. (1) At Lardarello, in Italy, steam accumulates in solution cavities in limestone and reaches the surface in wells at a temperature of about 230°C and pressures of 25 atmospheres. A body of hot igneous rock below the reservoirs is presumed to furnish the heat. Power production began in the 1930s. (2) Production of electricity from natural steam began at Reykjavik, Iceland, in 1964. (3) Wairakei, New Zealand, began generation of electricity from steam heated by volcanic rock in 1950. (4) The Geysers, in the Mayacmas Mountains, about 90 highway miles north of San Francisco, California (Figure 7-1), was first a health and recreation spa, and then in 1921, drilling and experimentation led to the generation of power. This was commercially successful by 1960, and remains the only commercial development of geothermal power in the United States, in spite of intensive exploration in recent years.

Figure 7-1 Looking northwest along Big Sulfur Creek, Sonoma County, at turbine-generator unit No. 3 (27,500 kilowatts) of power plant at The Geysers. Natural steam, blowing from wells in the background, is conducted through the gathering line to the generator (right), barometric condenser (center), and cooling towers (left). Heterogeneous rocks of the Franciscan Formation underlie and crop out in these Coast Range hills. Pacific Gas and Electric Company photo. (*Reproduced from Gordon B. Oakeshott,* California's Changing Landscapes, *by permission of McGraw-Hill Book Company.*)

The name "The Geysers" is a misnomer as only hot springs—not geysers—are known in the region. By 1974, about 400,000 kilowatts of electricity were being generated from 120 wells and 10 power plant units. This is enough to supply the power needs of a city of about 350,000 people. Superheated, dry steam is produced at temperatures of about 180°C and pressures of 9 or 10 atmospheres. The source of the heat is undoubtedly bodies of magma or hot volcanic rock associated with the geologically young Clear Lake rhyolitic volcanic rocks which are exposed a few miles away and which presumably underlie the much older reservoir rocks. Wells are up to 4,000 feet in depth, but none has yet penetrated these hot or perhaps molten volcanic materials.

SUMMARY
The wonderland of geysers, hot springs, and fumaroles in Yellowstone National Park is the greatest and best-known large area of the late stages of

declining volcanism anywhere in the world. Old Faithful is the world's best-known geyser. Yellowstone has been extensively studied by geologists, and field observations and studies continue today. Its geologic history is known back to 2 million years ago.

What do you think of the hypothesis that the rhyolites of Yellowstone represent the exposed top of a granite batholith? Why?

With the decline of the world's petroleum reserves, new sources of energy are being eagerly sought. One of these sources is natural steam from hot springs, geysers, and drilled wells. We are finding, however, that only a small proportion of known hot-spring areas has the special conditions, which we named in this chapter, that make for commercial development of the use of natural steam for energy. Many private companies and governments are currently (1975) prospecting for sources of steam for electrical energy.

After carefully reviewing Chapter 7, how would you prospect for sources of geothermal energy? That is, what geologic and other conditions would you consider favorable to making the investment necessary to drill a well to demonstrate a commercial source of natural steam?

Obviously, we might drill in a hot-spring or geyser area, and we might explore in areas of declining and late-stage volcanism. But consider that California, for example, has hundreds of hot springs; but so far only The Geysers is commercially successful, and this area remains the only current source of geothermal power in the United States. If you can come up with a list of prospecting criteria that greatly increases the chances of successfully prospecting for steam for power, your services will be greatly in demand!

EIGHT

FOUR BILLION YEARS OF VOLCANISM

Viewed in the broadest sense, the earth is a mass of igneous rock which is superficially covered, here and there, by thin layers of sediments.

So, how long has volcanism gone on? From the beginning—perhaps $4\frac{1}{2}$ billion years ago (Chapter 1)! When did the first volcanoes erupt? Probably as soon as the first earth crust was formed—perhaps 4 billion years ago.

During this vast length of time it is likely that the earth was never free from volcanic action, although volcanism waxed and waned and appeared at a maximum from time to time over different parts of the earth's surface.

Let us take a quick look at volcanism through the ages, beginning with the vast segment of geologic time called the Precambrian—from 4 billion to 600 million years ago (Table 1-1).

Every continent has a large area of exposed Precambrian rocks, called the *continental shield*. In North America the Canadian Shield covers most of eastern Canada and extends into the Great Lakes area and New York State. Within the Canadian Shield—and in all other continental shield areas of the earth—examination of the rocks shows that there were, at times, vast outpourings of flood basalts to build up areas of plateau lavas and, at other times, volcanic belts which were probably similar to modern volcanic arcs such as the Philippines or Japan. Some of these latter rocks show "pillow" structures, indicating eruption under the seas, and many of the rocks are volcanic breccias, clearly resulting from explosive eruptions. In the Canadian Shield, the oldest Precambrian volcanic rocks include a variety of types.

Younger Precambrian rocks in the Lake Superior region—about 1.1 billion years old—include vast amounts of rock from basalt flows which covered thousands of square miles and may have been as much as 25,000 feet thick. This accumulation is similar to the much younger Columbia River Plateau which we studied in Chapter 5. In many of the shield areas of the earth, there has been no volcanism since Precambrian time. Great uplift and subsequent erosion have exposed Precambrian rocks in the depths of mountain ranges. Again, these contain large proportions of volcanic rocks.

The Paleozoic Era—from about 600 to 225 million years ago—seems to have been quieter; for example, Cambrian rocks are nearly all of marine sedimentary origin. Such strata are beautifully and spectacularly exposed in the Canadian Rockies. But that is not to say that in those times there was not volcanism on some part of the earth's surface. In Europe, there was considerable volcanic activity at the close of the Cambrian period. In North America, important mountain building, accompanied by volcanism, took place in all the subsequent periods of the Paleozoic Era—Late Ordovician Taconic Mountains of the northeastern Appalachian area; Devonian Acadian Mountains in the same general area; and extensive mountain building and volcanism increasing from the Late Mississippian Period to the close of the Paleozoic Era in many parts of the continent. This seems to have been the broad pattern of activity in other continents of the earth, also.

The Mesozoic (225 to 70 million years ago) was an era of great volcanism, although its intensity and location varied greatly from time to time. Here are just a few highlights to illustrate what we mean.

Extensive thin flows and sheets (sills and dikes) of Late Triassic basalt show that fissure eruptions were widespread in eastern North America. Among the most noted Triassic outcrops are the Palisades along the Hudson River in New York.

The Jurassic period was a time of great mountain building, particularly in western North America. The Sierra Nevada and Coast Ranges of California, the Cascade Range of Washington and British Columbia, and many others, were folded, elevated, and intruded by granitic magmas; volcanism accompanied and followed this sort of activity. The Precambrian shield in southern Brazil was rent by fissures from which erupted extensive flood basalts in Cretaceous time. Eruptions of flood basalts in the Deccan Plateau in west central India covered an area close to 200,000 square miles in late Cretaceous and earliest Tertiary time. This was one of the great volcanic events in earth history.

Late Cretaceous to early Tertiary time saw the most important mountain building in the western Americas, extending from Alaska to the southern tip of South America and inland 1,000 miles to include the Rocky Mountains. In this vast area of mountain ranges the principal type of igneous activity was the intrusion of tremendous bodies of granitic magma to form batholiths, but andesitic-to-rhyolitic volcanism was also characteristic.

We cannot leave Mesozoic volcanism without mention of the oldest volcanic *forms* that exist on the earth today. About 1,000 volcanic islands dot the Pacific Ocean, many of which are active volcanoes. Many which are inactive have been eroded and are presently capped by coral limestone. But at least 10,000 more volcanic islands—rising 3,000 feet above the ocean floor—are not high enough to reach the surface of the water. These are the *seamounts*. Marine geologists now estimate that there are possibly 100,000 volcanic peaks on the deep, abyssal, ocean plains. These hills on the deep ocean floor have the conical forms of volcanic peaks, and many include craters. Many are as old as 100 million years! Nowhere on earth—except in the abyssal depths of the ocean—can landforms as old as these be preserved from destruction by erosion.

The 70 million years of the Cenozoic Era is a saga of intermittent volcanism—volcanism focused in areas of active mountain building, but more particularly at the margins of the earth's tectonic plates, plus certain hot spots of the ocean basins. It was in the late Mesozoic Era that the modern cycle of sea-floor spreading and plate movements began, with the beginning of formation of the present ocean basins, according to theories of plate tectonics (Chapter 3). The vast outpouring of lava to form the Columbia River Plateau (Chapter 5) in mid-to-late Miocene time was doubtless an effect related to sea-floor spreading.

All of the world's majestic and beautiful volcanic peaks are no older than the Pliocene Epoch—say, not over 3 million years old. Erosion has reduced older ones to volcanic necks, or to nothing but volcanic rocks which testify to their former existence.

Thus, the living testimony of volcanic cones and domes takes us back a few million years, that of abyssal oceanic hills a hundred million years; but evidence in the rocks tells the story of volcanism from the very dawn of earth history!

Are we living in times of any less volcanic activity than in the past?

Probably not. For any comparable time in earth history we can see no evidence that the worldwide volcanism of all types and forms was ever exceeded or matched in 4 billion years of geologic history. We are indeed living in volcanic times!

SUMMARY

Volcanic activity has gone on somewhere on the surface of the earth in all geologic periods since the beginning, over 4 billion years ago. Careful studies of the volcanic rock formations, which reveal when, where, and what kind of volcanism took place, have been made in most parts of the earth.

From ancient rock formations we can tell much about the type of volcanism that went on. Why is this true?

Some questions to think about: How can we tell the direction of prevailing winds in some places millions of years ago? Were there volcanoes in Precambrian time? Were they more numerous than they are today? What can ancient volcanic rocks tell us of the locations of long-gone boundaries of moving crustal plates? Do volcanic rocks ever preserve fossils? How?

List all the features of their environment that volcanic *rocks* could tell us something about. Look up seamounts to learn more about those strange submarine peaks. In any historical geology textbook, look up the Precambrian shield areas of the earth—those low-lying regions of the continents where there has been no volcanism for at least the last 600 million years. How are the Precambrian shields related to the continents on the earth and to present-day tectonic plates?

NINE

OBSERVATIONS OF A GREAT EARTHQUAKE
AND THE FEATURES OF FAULTS

OWENS VALLEY, CALIFORNIA, EARTHQUAKE OF 1872

At half past two o'clock of a moon-lit morning in March, I was awakened by a
tremendous earthquake, and though I had never before enjoyed a storm of
this sort, the strange thrilling motion could not be mistaken, and I ran out of
my cabin, both glad and frightened, shouting, "A noble earthquake!" feeling
sure I was going to learn something. The shocks were so violent and varied,
and succeeded one another so closely, that I had to balance myself
carefully in walking as if on the deck of a ship among waves, and it seemed
impossible that the high cliffs of the Valley could escape being shattered. In
particular, I feared that the sheer-fronted Sentinel Rock, towering above my
cabin, would be shaken down, and I took shelter back of a large yellow pine,
hoping that it might protect me from at least the smaller outbounding
boulders. For a minute or two the shocks became more and more violent—
flashing horizontal thrusts mixed with a few twists and battering, explosive,
upheaving jolts—as if Nature were wrecking her Yosemite temple, and
getting ready to build a still better one.

It was a calm moonlight night, and no sound was heard for the first
minute or so, save low, muffled, underground bubbling rumblings, and the
whispering and rustling of the agitated trees, as if Nature were holding her
breath. Then, suddenly, out of the strange silence and strange motion there
came a tremendous roar. The Eagle Rock on the south wall, about a half a
mile up the Valley, gave way and I saw it falling in thousands of great
boulders I had so long been studying, pouring to the Valley floor in a free
curve luminous from friction, making a terribly sublime spectacle—an arc of

Figure 9-1 The tremendous fault scarp of the Fairview Peak, central Nevada, earthquake of December 1954. Where the scarp crosses the ridge, near the upper left corner, roots of pinon trees were displaced 7 feet vertically and 11 feet horizontally—upthrown block toward the viewer. (*Scratchboard drawing by Peter H. Oakeshott, from a kodachrome.*)

glowing, passionate fire, fifteen hundred feet span, as true in form and as serene in beauty as a rainbow in the midst of the stupendous, roaring rock-storm. The sound was so tremendously deep and broad and earnest, the whole earth like a living creature seemed to have at last found a voice and to be calling her sister planets. In trying to tell something of the size of this awful sound it seems to me that if all the thunder of all the storms I had ever heard were condensed into one roar it would not equal this rock-roar at the birth of a mountain talus.

Thus, the great naturalist and preservationist, John Muir, wrote of his experience in Yosemite Valley in the Owens Valley earthquake of March 26, 1872. Although at first frightened as he was awakened in his cabin at the foot of Sentinel Rock that early morning, he gloried in the sounds, shaking, and falls of rock loosened from the 3,000-foot-high granite walls of Yosemite Valley. A keen observer, he left one of the few competent eyewitness accounts of that earthquake—certainly one of California's three greatest earthquakes—and its aftershocks.

Near the epicenter, the town of Lone Pine, in Owens Valley in Inyo County at the eastern foot of the Sierra Nevada, had a population of 250 to

300 persons in 1872. They were mostly Mexicans who had brought with them the practice of building adobe and stone houses, usually without any kind of mortar. Lumber was scarce and relatively expensive. These houses were "crumbled and went to earth like piles of sand, burying the miserable occupants in the ruins. . . ." So reported the local *Inyo Independent* of April 6, 1872. At Lone Pine, 23 dead were listed (almost 10 percent of the population!) and at least 50 people were injured.

What had happened on that early morning of March 26, 1872?

Extensive surface faulting and ground rupturing had taken place in Owens Valley along a portion of the Sierra Nevada fault zone for a distance of nearly 100 miles and a width across the valley of less than 1 to 10 miles. In geological time a century is but a moment, and so to this day, the greatest ruptures remain clear from Haiwee to Big Pine; uncertain ruptures were developed from Big Pine to Bishop (Figure 9-2). In terms of length of faulting, this is the third greatest in California history. The length of the fault break in the 1906 San Francisco earthquake was 270 miles, while Fort Tejon in 1857 was about 225 miles.

In the 1857 and 1906 earthquakes, displacement along the faults was almost entirely horizontal, a maximum perhaps as much as 30 feet in 1857 and 20 feet in 1906. Maximum vertical surface displacement just northwest of Lone Pine in 1872 was 23 feet in alluvial fan materials; but there was also a horizontal component of displacement of 16 feet. A graben, or fault trough, a few hundred feet wide was formed between the high east-facing scarp and a 10-foot west-facing scarp. Thus, the net vertical displacement at Lone Pine

Figure 9-2 Eroded Owens Valley fault scarp 100 years after the earthquake of 1872, near Lone Pine. This may have been California's greatest earthquake. (*California Division of Mines and Geology.*)

was 13 feet. Elsewhere along much of the Sierra Nevada fault zone there is little evidence for anything but vertical movement.

Because of a scarcity of people in California, and very few geologists, first hand accounts of the 1872 earthquake and fault zone are extremely rare. State Geologist J. D. Whitney visited the earthquake zone in May 1872 and published two papers later that year describing the damage and faulting, but he failed to note whether the Sierra Nevada mountain block had been displaced relatively northward or southward! W. D. Johnson, of the U.S. Geological Survey, visited the Valley in 1907, drew some excellent sketch maps, and showed clearly that the Sierran block had indeed moved relatively northward. But faulting was complex and the pattern of faults in the Valley involved both vertical and horizontal displacement. Fracturing of the earth, local settling of the ground surface, and grabens were extensive and widespread over the valley floor. Also, on a midvalley trace of the fault, several feet of horizontal movement in an opposite direction to that at Lone Pine took place. Geologic evidence shows that the Sierra Nevada has been repeatedly uplifted along the faults on the east side of the mountains (the west side of Owens Valley) for a total of several thousands of feet during Quaternary time.

What about seismological data on the Owens Valley earthquake?

Seismological data are scant for this great earthquake. Seismographs were not introduced until 1887, and no one had reported any systematic records of foreshocks and aftershocks. The railroads were the first to adopt standard time belts across the United States, but this did not apply to California until 1883; even then there were no precise time signals until 1887, when Lick Observatory began furnishing them, in the same year in which it installed seismographs. Thus, time comparisons across the state were uncertain and inaccurate. At the time of day (2:30 A.M.) when the earthquake occurred, most people were asleep, and so personal accounts were unreliable, incomplete, or lacking.

Probably there were some foreshocks, smaller shocks occurring before the big one. Historians report a "shock of some severity" at Lone Pine on March 17, 1872, and records list a number from one end of Owens Valley to the other in July 1871. There can be no doubt of the aftershocks which were widely felt for months after the great earthquake. Three severe aftershocks followed on the morning of the 26th, for instance, and on May 17, Lone Pine experienced the "most severe since the great shock of March 26." Seismologists can do little to analyze the aftershock sequence with the sporadic and conflicting reports which make up the record.

How big was it? The Owens Valley earthquake is generally believed to be the greatest on record in the western United States, excluding Alaska; yet, there is a surprising lack of information in the technical literature concerning its effects. Ground shaking was felt throughout most of California and Nevada, in Oregon and Arizona, and as far away as Salt Lake City, Utah. A great many newspapers in California and Nevada carried descriptions of the effects of the shaking in their localities. It was reported that one of the iron columns of the Capitol building in Sacramento was broken. Coastal communities in California, from San Diego to Eureka, experienced intensities from IV to VI; in Los Angeles, some people were thrown from their beds and most ran into the streets.

Because the earthquake occurred before the advent of the seismograph, there is no direct (i.e., instrumental) way of determining its Richter magnitude. However, magnitude can be estimated from the size of the area over which an earthquake is felt, or from the average epicentral distance to a given isoseismal line, and from the length of the surface fault zone. Felt area is difficult to determine for this shock, but the size of the felt area, from old newspaper accounts, roughly corresponds to a Richter magnitude around 8. Comparisons with the well-known Alaskan earthquake of 1964 (magnitude 8.5) and the San Francisco earthquake of 1906 (magnitude 8.3) suggest that Owens Valley 1872 may have had a magnitude of at least 8.3.

What is the recurrence rate of great earthquakes—like that of 1872—along the eastern Sierra Nevada front? We have no evidence for any regular periodicity of earthquakes, but geologists and seismologists judge that strains build up in that area to the point of major rupture every few hundred years. Geologic evidence is overwhelming that uplift of the Sierra Nevada is actively continuing. The "noble" earthquake that John Muir felt in 1872 and that killed so many people in Lone Pine was clearly due to but one episode of many displacements along the great Sierra Nevada fault zone. There is every reason to expect more big earthquakes originating on this fault in the future.

FAULTING AND TYPES OF FAULT MOVEMENT

Clearly, the Owens Valley earthquake was a series of complex ground vibrations set up by displacements along the Sierra Nevada fault zone. The immediate and direct cause of the earthquake was abrupt breaking and displacement along a near-vertical fault surface. There is geological evidence that repeated fault breaks have occurred in the same fault zone over a period of perhaps 3 million years. Faulting is a normal process of mountain building. Rocks of the earth's crust are elastic and they yield to mountain-building stresses by slow strain or distortion over long periods of time. When the elastic limit of the rock material is reached at any point, or friction along an old fault surface is overcome, an abrupt displacement and rebound take place. This sets up earthquake vibrations. The focus (Chapter 1) of an earthquake is the point—usually at least a few kilometers below the surface of the earth—at which the initial break appears to take place. From that point, the fault rupture spreads upward and in horizontal directions at a rate on the order of 2 kilometers per second to define a fault surface. Most destructive earthquakes have shallow focuses—not over 40 kilometers (25 miles). Many, like those in California earthquakes, are less than 15 kilometers deep.

The fault surface is often called the *fault plane*; but what is it really like? We can learn something about this from studying the fault line on the ground surface and from seismograph records, both of which yield data allowing the seismologist to figure out *dip* (angle of inclination of the fault plane to the horizontal) and *strike* (direction) of the fault plane. Such fault measurements have been made in many earthquakes and have shown that, while many fault surfaces approach a plane, many are curved, warped, or broken. For

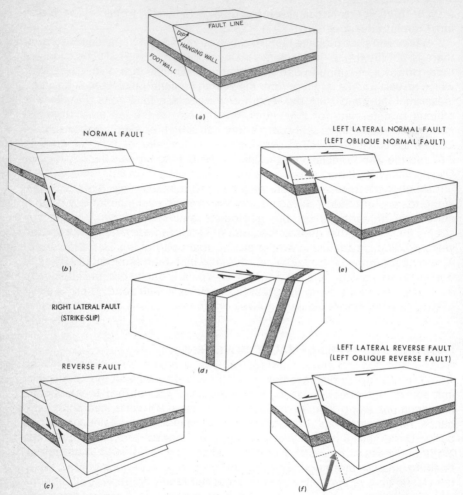

Figure 9-3 Types of fault movement or displacement. (*California Division of Mines and Geology.*)

example, in the San Fernando 1971 earthquake, the initial break was about 8 kilometers deep with a fault surface dipping about 55°; but the rupture projected upward at lower and lower angles, finally reaching the surface at an angle of less than 20° with the horizontal plane. Not only was the fault surface curved, but it was also so sharply warped that the strike of the fault at the ground surface changed abruptly several times along a trace which extended about 12 miles. A fault surface along which movement takes place is often marked by the development of broken rock and claylike powdered rock. Such surfaces may be seen when erosion has exposed an ancient fault.

Faulting takes place in all kinds of rock and displacement occurring at any one time may be anything from a fraction of an inch to several feet. Along the course of a major fault, repeated small displacements—with or without resulting earthquakes—may take place at irregular intervals over long periods of geologic time until the cumulative displacement may amount to many miles. In such situations the fault becomes a fault *zone* of shattered and broken rock that may be more than a mile in width, often with rock formations of widely different type, structure, and age brought into contact with each other.

A fault surface may dip at any angle from the horizontal to the vertical, and relative displacement of the opposite blocks along the fault may be horizontal, vertical, or any combination of these. The actual displacement of a point in a fault plane is called the *slip*. In some faults the character of the displacement may change along the strike and also may change in geologic time. Figure 9-3 shows the principal fault types, fault movements, and fault nomenclature.

(a) An unfaulted block with a horizontal bed or stratum (stippled) and an incipient fault. The strike of the fault is the compass direction of the "fault line" in the diagram. Remember that the dip of the fault might be anything from 0 to 90°.

(b) A *normal* fault, in which the *hanging wall* (the side "on top" of a dipping fault plane) has moved down with respect to the *footwall* (the side "on the bottom" of a dipping fault plane). This is a *tensional* fault because the movement tends to lengthen the earth's surface across the fault.

(c) A *reverse* fault, in which the hanging wall has moved up relative to the footwall. When the dip of the fault plane becomes less than 45° in a reverse fault it is called a *thrust* fault. Reverse and thrust faults are compressional; they shorten the earth's surface across the fault. In normal and reverse faults, the slip is *dip slip*, or mainly an "up and down" or vertical movement.

(d) A *lateral* or *strike-slip* fault, in which slip is horizontal along the strike of the fault. This one is *left-lateral* because the fault block opposite the observer, as the observer faces the fault, has moved to the left. *Right-lateral* faults are equally common.

(e) This combines left-lateral and normal fault components to make a *left-lateral normal fault*. Displacement is by *oblique slip* (arrow).

(f) Combines left-lateral and reverse components to make a *left-lateral reverse fault*. Again, displacement is by oblique slip (arrow).

SUMMARY

In Chapter 9, we reviewed what is known about one of the world's great earthquakes of the last century. We quoted an eyewitness account from a point about 100 miles away from the epicenter.

Note the things of scientific interest that John Muir's account of the Owens Valley earthquake, as felt and observed in Yosemite Valley, tells us.

How big was the Owens Valley earthquake? No seismograms are available, so we have no measured magnitude, but we still have at least two important kinds of information on which to base some judgments of the size of this earthquake. What are they?

We have used the Owens Valley earthquake—with its strong evidence of complex surface faulting—as a way to introduce faulting, the types of fault movement or displacement which may occur, and fault nomenclature. Some important things to remember: (1) The fault surface, or fault plane, on which slippage occurs may be at any angle, from horizontal to vertical; (2) this angle may change along the strike of a fault; (3) the fault surface is often curved or irregular, and it may be grooved, striated, and scratched, thus showing the direction of movement; (4) fault movement (displacement) may be anything from a fraction of an inch to several feet during one earthquake (Chapter 10).

Geologists judgé that an earthquake like that of Owens Valley in 1872 occurs, due to faulting in the Sierra Nevada fault zone, every several hundred years. What evidence is there for this sort of forecast?

One of the world's greatest earthquakes (Lisbon, 1755; see Chapter 12) may have had a magnitude as high as 8.9. Can you think of reasons why no earthquake may exceed this magnitude?

TEN

THE SAN ANDREAS FAULT SYSTEM,
ITS EARTHQUAKE HISTORY,
AND THE ELASTIC REBOUND THEORY

One of the world's greatest and most widely known faults is the San Andreas Fault, stretching for 600 miles obliquely across California's Coast and Transverse Ranges from near Cape Mendocino to the Salton Sea (Figures 10-1 and 10-2). Historic movements on this fault have not been largely vertical, like the Sierra Nevada and Hebgen faults, but have been horizontal, with the east block moving relatively south. In the San Francisco earthquake of 1906 the maximum movement offset a dirt road at Tomales Bay over 20 feet, and in 1857 the horizontal offset in the remote southeastern part of the Coast Ranges was perhaps as much as 30 feet. Countless movements of this type over millions of years have created a striking series of almost-straight *rift valleys* roughly parallel to California's north-northwesterly–trending coastline. Straight, shallow Tomales Bay—1 mile wide and 15 miles long—lies in the rift zone north of San Francisco; and just south of Tomales the rift zone is a steep-sided trough as deep as 1,500 feet, including a most remarkable succession of minor, alternating ridges and gullies parallel to the general trend of the fault zone. Many of the hollows in the rift zone are undrained and form the ponds so common along the length of the San Andreas Fault. On the San Francisco Peninsula the rift valley is occupied by the long and narrow Crystal Springs Lakes. These and other features of the San Andreas fault zone have resulted from (1) repeated, discontinuous fault ruptures on the surface over millions of years, often with the development of minor fault

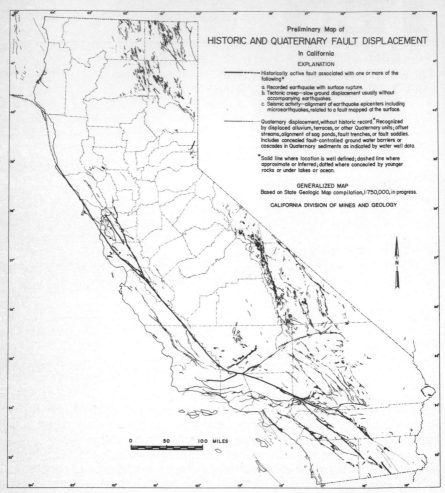

Figure 10-1 Historic and Quaternary fault displacements in California. Major fault system is the San Andreas. At its north end, the San Andreas Fault merges westward into the submarine Mendocino Escarpment; in the San Francisco Bay Area the San Andreas system includes the Hayward and Calaveras Faults; and in the south the fault system splits into the Newport-Inglewood Fault (on the coast), the Elsinore Fault, the San Jacinto Fault, and the San Andreas Fault proper, west to east. The complex Sierra Nevada fault zone is seen on the east side of the southern Sierra Nevada. The major northeast-trending fault is the Garlock; paralleling the Garlock Fault and a few miles north of it, is the active White Wolf Fault which caused the Arvin-Tehachapi earthquake of 1952.

depressions, or graben; (2) landsliding, triggered by earthquake shaking and surface faulting; and (3) erosion of broken, readily weathered rock.

Few specific geologic features on earth have received more public attention. Sound reasons for this are found in the series of historic earthquakes which have been caused by movements in the San Andreas fault zone, and in continuing surface displacements both accompanied and unaccompanied by earthquakes. This active fault is of tremendous engineering significance, for no engineering structure can be built across it without jeopardy. All major structures built within its potential area of seismicity must incorporate earthquake-resistant design features. Recently a proposal for a great nuclear power plant installation on Bodega Head, north of San Francisco, was abandoned because of public controversy over the dangers of renewed movements and earthquakes on the nearby San Andreas Fault. Expensive design features have been incorporated into the state's plan to transport some of northern California's excess of water to water-deficient southern California, in order to ensure uninterrupted service across the fault in the event of fault movements and earthquakes in the Tehachapi area.

Geologists and seismologists the world over have directed their attention to the San Andreas Fault because of: (1) the great (Richter magnitude 8.3) San Francisco earthquake of 1906 and many lesser shocks which have originated in the fault zone; (2) development of the *elastic rebound* theory of earthquakes (see below) by H. F. Reid; (3) striking geologic effects of former movements and continuing surface movements in the fault zone; and (4)

Figure 10-2 The San Andreas Fault cuts through the northern Temblor Range. View is toward the north. (*John S. Shelton, courtesy of California Division of Mines and Geology.*)

postulated horizontal displacements of hundreds of miles, the east block moving relatively south.

The San Andreas has been frequently and widely cited in the scientific and popular literature as a classic example of a strike-slip fault, with a cumulative horizontal displacement of several hundred miles; however, geologic evidence shows that it has had important vertical displacement as well.

LOCATION AND EXTENT
The San Andreas Fault trends north-northwest in a nearly straight line in the Coast Ranges of California and extends southward for a total length of about 600 miles from the coast of Humboldt County in northern California to the Salton Sea in southeastern California. This takes it completely across the geologic structures of the Coast Ranges at a low angle, then south across the Transverse Ranges and into the Salton Sea basin.

GEOLOGY OF THE FAULT ZONE
The Coast Ranges province is a series of north-northwest–trending mountain ranges and intermontane valleys bounded on the east by the Great Valley and on the West by the Pacific Ocean. Since the San Andreas Fault trends slightly more to the west than the general trend of the province, the fault zone completely crosses the Coast Ranges from its suboceanic junction with the Mendocino Escarpment off the north coast of California to the foothills on the western margin of the San Joaquin Valley in the south. The fault zone therefore crosses all essential elements of the extremely complex geology of the Coast Ranges. In that province, it generally separates two regions consisting of entirely different "basement" rocks—the granitic and metamorphic rocks of the Sur Series, from the great thickness of marine sedimentary and volcanic rocks of the Franciscan Formation.

In 1953, California petroleum geologists Mason L. Hill and T. W. Dibblee, Jr., advanced the possibility of cumulative horizontal displacement of possibly 350 miles since Jurassic time (135 million years ago) on the San Andreas Fault. The block of land west of the fault has moved northward relative to the east block. This hypothesis received very wide acceptance among earth scientists and has helped to stimulate work on the fault. Hill and Dibblee compared rock types, fossils, and gradational changes in rock characteristics in attempting to match units across the fault. By these methods they developed suggestions for horizontal displacement (east block moving south) of 10 miles since the Pleistocene (11,000 years), 65 miles since upper Miocene (about 12 million years), 225 miles since late Eocene (about 40 million years), and 350 miles since the Jurassic. This was long before the popular trend in thinking on continental drift and sea-floor spreading, so many geologists felt less confident about this matching of rock units and stated that principal movements on the great fault had been vertical. There can be no question that both important strike-slip and vertical movements have taken place on the fault repeatedly in Quaternary time—the last 3 million years. Most contemporary geologists subscribe to the theory that the San Andreas Fault separates the northwestward-moving oceanic Pacific plate from the relatively southeastward-moving continental North American plate.

LAND FORMS IN THE FAULT ZONE

Extensive activity along the San Andreas fault zone in Quaternary time has developed a linear depression, marked by all the features of a classic rift valley, extending the entire length of the fault and encompassing a width ranging from a few hundred feet to over $1\frac{1}{2}$ miles. Rift-valley features are particularly well expressed in the San Francisco Bay Area, in the arid Carrizo Plain, in the southern Coast Ranges (Figure 10-2), and along the north side of the Transverse Ranges in southern California. Within the rift zone broken and powdered rock are present, the result of hundreds of repeated ruptures on different fault planes in late Pleistocene and Holocene time. Features of the rift valleys have resulted from (1) repeated, discontinuous fault ruptures on the surface, often with blocks of rock either being lowered or raised; (2) landsliding, triggered by earthquake waves and surface faulting; and (3) erosion of broken, readily weathered rock. Within the rift-valley troughs, it is common to find geologically young sediments.

Many of the observations made after the earthquake of 1906 are of great significance in understanding the origin and development of rift valleys as well as the nature of movement on the San Andreas fault: (1) open ruptures were mapped along the fault trace for 225 miles in northern California; (2) individual fault ruptures were not continuous, but extended for a few feet to a mile or a little more, with the continuations of the displacements being picked up along other parallel breaks; (3) the ruptures were often complex, with small down-dropped or uplifted blocks developed between breaks; (4) apparent movements were dominantly right-lateral, with lesser vertical displacements; and (5) the amount of displacement varied irregularly along the fault, but in a gross way decreased in both directions from the maximum of 20 feet at the south end of Tomales Bay, about 25 miles northwest of San Francisco.

In southern California, south of the Tehachapi Mountains, the striking rift-valley landforms continue, through sag ponds, across the desert, and along the northern margin of the Transverse Ranges and across their eastern end. None of the offsets and other rift-valley features along the southern segment of the great fault appears to have been formed since 1857.

EARTHQUAKE HISTORY

The earthquake history of California is extremely short. The earliest earthquake in written records was noted by explorer Gaspar de Portolá and his party in 1769. They felt the shocks while camped on the Santa Ana River about 30 miles southeast of Los Angeles. The earliest seismographs in use in California, and also the earliest in the United States, were installed by the University of California at Lick Observatory (on Mount Hamilton, southeast of San Francisco Bay) and at the University at Berkeley in 1887. The earliest

Figure 10-3 The San Francisco City Hall stands in an area of intense damage after the earthquake of April 18, 1906. (*Collection of the California Division of Mines and Geology.*)

seismograms of a major California earthquake are those of the San Francisco earthquake of 1906, which was recorded at seven California stations as well as elsewhere throughout the world.

One of the San Francisco Bay Area's largest earthquakes centered on the Hayward Fault (within the San Andreas fault *zone*) in the East Bay on June 10, 1836. Surface faulting (ground ruptures) took place at the base of the Berkeley Hills from Mission San Jose to San Pablo, a distance of 40 miles. On October 21, 1868, another large earthquake centered on the Hayward Fault with surface faulting for about 20 miles from Warm Springs to San Leandro (Oakland). Maximum offset was about 3 feet.

In June of 1838 a strong earthquake originating on the San Andreas Fault was accompanied by surface rupturing extending the length of the San Francisco Peninsula. This damaged the Presidio at San Francisco and the missions at San Jose, nearby Santa Clara, and San Francisco. Another strong earthquake centered on the San Andreas Fault in the Santa Cruz Mountains (south of the San Francisco Peninsula) on October 8, 1865. This was accompanied by ground cracks, landslides, and dust clouds; buildings were damaged in San Francisco and at the famous New Almaden mercury mine, which was only a few miles east of the active part of the fault.

On April 24, 1890, a strong earthquake damaged the small towns of Watsonville, Hollister, and Gilroy. In 1963, I interviewed Joe Anzar, who was a young boy living in the San Andreas rift valley in the nearby Chittenden Pass area in the Santa Cruz Mountains at the time of that earthquake. Mr. Anzar clearly remembered ground breakage, which caused Anzar Lake to drain, and landslides, which closed the railroad and highway where the fault trace crosses Chittenden Pass. He judged the motion to be stronger (at his home) than during the San Francisco earthquake of 1906.

The famous San Francisco earthquake, 5:12 A.M., local time, April 18, 1906, was one of California's three greatest (Figures 10-3 and 10-4). Visible surface faulting occurred for about 225 miles from San Juan Bautista to Point Arena in northern California, where the San Andreas Fault enters the ocean. At the same time surface faulting also occurred 75 miles north of Point Arena at Shelter Cove (on the coast near latitude 40°N) in Humboldt County, probably along an extension of the San Andreas Fault. Total length of surface faulting was about 270 miles. The 1906 scarp viewed at Shelter Cove in 1963 clearly shows upthrow of 6 to 8 feet on the east side; there was no evidence of a horizontal component of displacement. However, the offset of a line of old trees and an old fence viewed east of Point Arena in 1963 gave clear evidence of right-lateral displacement on the order of about 14 feet. The earthquake was centered on the San Andreas Fault west of San Francisco, close to the Golden Gate. Richter magnitude is generally computed at about 8.3. Damage has been estimated at from $350 million to $1 billion. An estimated 700 people were killed. A large part of the loss was due to tremendous fires in San

Figure 10-4 Typical street scene in San Francisco the morning after the earthquake of April 18, 1906. Because of broken gas mains and water lines fires raged unchecked through the city. (*Photo by W. E. Worden, in California Division of Mines and Geology collection. Reproduced from Gordon B. Oakeshott, California's Changing Landscapes, by permission of McGraw-Hill Book Company.*)

Francisco, which resulted from broken gas mains and lack of water owing to numerous ruptures in the lines. Most extensive ground breaking in the city was near the waterfront in areas of natural Bay mud and artificial fill.

Another of California's great earthquakes, comparable in magnitude to the San Francisco 1906 earthquake, was caused by displacement on a segment of the San Andreas Fault extending through the southern part of the Coast Ranges province and on beyond across the Transverse Ranges. This Fort Tejon earthquake of January 9, 1857, probably centered in the region between Fort Tejon in the Tehachapi Mountains and the Carrizo Plain in the southern Coast Ranges. Surface faulting extended for 200 to 275 miles. Accounts of this earthquake are unsatisfactory and inconclusive, but it is apparent that horizontal displacement may have amounted to 30 feet near the epicenter.

There have been in historic times two great earthquakes (Fort Tejon and San Francisco) originating on the San Andreas Fault, each accompanied by more than 200 miles of surface ruptures; one occurred at the southern end of the Coast Ranges and one in the north. Between is left a segment, roughly 90 miles long, which has not been disrupted by surface faulting in a major earthquake in historic time. It is interesting to note that the two ends of this segment—the Hollister area and the Parkfield area—are now the most seismically active in the southern Coast Ranges. The extreme southern segment of the fault is quiet on the San Andreas Fault proper, but very active on the closely related San Jacinto, Elsinore, Inglewood, and Imperial Faults. In the segment marked by surface rupture in 1906, many earthquakes have originated in the central and southern part on the San Andreas Fault and its auxiliary faults in the East Bay—the Hayward and Calaveras Faults. However, since 1906 there have been no earthquakes on the most northerly segment from Marin County to Humboldt County.

The strongest earthquake in the Bay Area since 1906 was the San

Figure 10-5 Displacement of a line by horizontal movement along the San Andreas Fault in 1906. The line B'BB' represents the trace of the fault. ABC is a straight line before strain or fault movement. A'BC' is the line strained by crustal movement. The lines A'B' and B'C' show the situation after fault rupture and total displacement B'B'. *(Adapted from H. F. Reid, Report of the State Earthquake Investigation Commission, vol. 11, 1910.)*

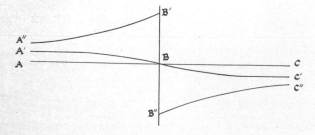

Francisco earthquake of March 22, 1957, of magnitude 5.3. It originated at shallow depth near Mussel Rock, off the coast a few miles south of San Francisco; there was no surface faulting. No lives were lost, but minor damage to many homes on the mainland totaled about $1 million.

THE ELASTIC REBOUND THEORY

Only three days after the great San Francisco earthquake, the Governor of California appointed a State Earthquake Investigation Commission. Headed by A. C. Lawson, Professor of Geology at the University of California, the Commission established a model for earthquake investigation and issued a monumental, profusely illustrated report[1]—Volume I on the geology, surface effects, intensities, and damage, and Volume II on the mechanics of the earthquake.

The author of Volume II—Harry Fielding Reid of Johns Hopkins University—expressed a whole new concept of the mechanism of faulting (Figure 10-5). Two or three decades earlier, geologists had begun to recognize that large earthquakes were sometimes accompanied by faulting, but they had visualized the earthquakes as causing the fault breaks. Then, in 1891, the Japanese scientist B. Koto investigated a great earthquake in his country which was accompanied by offset roads and fences along a 95-kilometer surface break. Koto recognized the earthquake as the *result* of the faulting and proposed such faulting as the cause of earthquakes. This was a startling new idea to seismologists and geologists, but the San Francisco, 1906, earthquake strongly reinforced the new theory.

After the great earthquake of 1906, Reid reexamined survey data of the U.S. Coast and Geodetic Survey across the San Andreas Fault in the San Francisco Bay Area. He compared lengths of lines across the fault measured from 1851 to 1865 and from 1874 to 1892 with postearthquake measurements during 1906 and 1907. The data were clear: points west of the fault had generally moved several feet northward with respect to points east of the fault! Reid concluded that rocks across the fault had been bent elastically, or strained, until the stresses causing the strains had exceeded the strength of the rocks; then the rocks had ruptured, snapping elastically forward to a new position of no stress or strain. (Reid's diagram is shown in Figure 10-5.) This he called the *elastic rebound theory*.

The principles of the elastic rebound theory are generally recognized today, but we can go a little further (Figure 10-6). The main shock relieves much, but not all, of the stress. A break along a fault may just shift some strain to another point where stress is again relieved—by an aftershock—and so on until regional strain has been reduced. Aftershocks may also result from a sort of "stick-slip" mechanism; that is, a slip along a fault

[1]"The California earthquake of April 18, 1906," *Report of the State Earthquake Commission: Carnegie Institution of Washington*, vol. I, 1908, and vol. II, 1910. The report was reprinted in 1969 and is available from the Carnegie Institution, Washington, D.C., for $12.50.

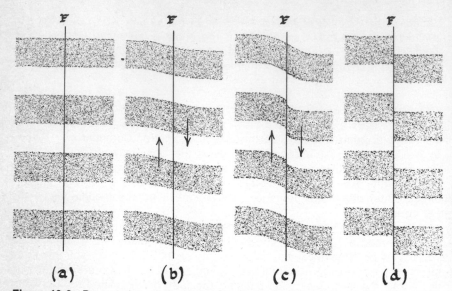

Figure 10-6 Propagation of displacement along a fault (see, also, Reid, Figure 10-5). The line F is the straight trace of a fault like the San Andreas Fault. (*a*) The position of no strain and no displacement; (*b*) Strain is occurring and the right side is moving horizontally in a right-lateral sense; (*c*) Strength of the rock is being exceeded and faulting is beginning and is being propagated in both directions; and (*d*) The fault displacement has been completed and a position of no strain has been reached. Diagram adapted from elastic rebound and strain-release theories.

surface is checked by friction, the fault "sticks," and then another slip occurs. Seismologists know a lot today about patterns of stress relief in earthquakes.

SUMMARY

The great San Francisco earthquake of 1906 advanced our knowledge of earthquakes tremendously. Can you name several things we learned about earthquakes? Why is San Francisco, 1906, considered an earthquake of enormous significance and why can we say that "few specific geologic features on earth have received more public attention" than the San Andreas Fault?

What is the relationship between the San Andreas Fault and the California Aqueduct? What safety measures might be taken in constructing an aqueduct across an active fault?

According to plate tectonic theory, the San Andreas Fault separates the relatively southeastward-moving North American crustal block from the northwestward-moving Pacific block. Have you developed any ideas on this (see Chapter 3 again)?

If you were walking along and across a great fault or rift zone—like the San Andreas—what landforms and other features of the landscape might you see that would convince you that you were in a fault zone?

ELEVEN

EARTHQUAKE WAVES AND THEIR EFFECTS

What did John Muir feel in Yosemite Valley in the early morning of March 26, 1872?

He tells of shocks which were "so violent and varied, and succeeded one another so closely, that I had to balance myself carefully in walking—flashing horizontal thrusts mixed with a few twists and battering, explosive, upheaving jolts. . . ."

Clearly, he felt the strong surface waves of that great earthquake.

THREE TYPES OF WAVES

Surface waves are one of three principal types of earthquake waves, the other two being *P waves*, which are the longitudinal, compressional, or "push-pull" type, and *S waves*, which are transverse or shear waves. As atoms in the rock exposed to the force of rupture push directly on their neighbors, particles are set to moving forward and backward, causing expansions and compressions of the material in the direction of propagation to generate the P wave, which is thus transmitted parallel to its line of propagation. (By noting on a seismogram the direction of first motion—and taking into account certain other factors—seismologists are able to calculate the dip and strike of the fault plane at depth.) In S waves, the particles move sideways and wave motion is transmitted in a shear fashion, transverse to the line of propagation.

Where the initial rupture on a fault takes place at the focus, the P and S waves start out together, but P waves move faster than S waves. Thus, P waves are the first or *primary* earthquake waves to arrive at a seismograph station and S waves are the *secondary* waves. P waves may move through rocks of the earth's crust at a speed of 6 to 8 kilometers per second; S waves move perhaps 3 to 4 kilometers per second; the P wave is the first to arrive. We can see, therefore, that the difference in time of arrival of P and S waves at a station is a measure of the distance of the earthquake from the seismograph station; the greater the distance the farther the S wave lags behind in time. A complicating factor is that both types of waves move faster in dense rock than they do in loose, low-density materials. Also, the S waves—being waves of *shear* or *distortion*—are not transmitted through fluids.

If we have accurate times of arrival of the P and S waves of a given earthquake at several favorably located seismograph stations, we can draw arcs of circles (the radius of each is the distance, computed from the difference in arrival time, to the source of the P and S waves) on a map, which should intersect at the earthquake epicenter, immediately above the earthquake focus at depth. To do this accurately we need to know precise travel times of the waves between focus and seismograph station. The same principles apply to finding the depth of the focus of an earthquake, but the seismograph stations must be favorably located, not too far away. P and S waves are sometimes felt (even *heard*, in unusual circumstances) by people and animals, but the S waves and particularly surface waves are the ones which cause the principal shaking which we call an earthquake. What are surface waves like?

Seismologists recognize two types of surface waves: *Love waves* and *Rayleigh waves*. Surface waves move more slowly than S waves. In the Love type, the motion of the ground is a *shearing motion* (as in the S wave), with no vertical motion and no compression or expansion. In Rayleigh waves, the motion is elliptical in a vertical plane parallel to the direction of propagation, with both vertical and horizontal components of displacement. Judging from his graphic description, John Muir evidently felt both Love and Rayleigh waves in their extremes!

This book is no place to discuss wave theory and wave analysis, but we should note that everything happens to earthquake waves that happens to other kinds of waves: They may be reflected and refracted (bent) in moving from one material to another; their amplitudes (heights) and frequencies may change; they become "weakened" or attenuated with distance, and certain types of waves may die out, selectively.

RECORDING EARTHQUAKE WAVES
How are earthquake waves recorded?

The seismograph (Figure 11-1) is the instrument used to record earthquake waves, and the record it makes is the seismogram (Figure 11-2). The thing we wish to record, of course, is the motion of the earth. This is not so easy to do, mechanically. We need some kind of suspended, heavy mass which is free to move relative to the ground and which is virtually "unconnected" with the ground (a skyhook would be ideal), so that when the ground shakes, the mass remains still. A pendulum is such a free mass, and all seismographs—sophisticated as some may be—depend for their operation on the principle of the pendulum. Next, we need some kind of device equipped with a pen to transfer the motions of the pendulum to the seismogram. Now, if the seismogram is moved at a regular rate on a rotating drum by a clock we should get a timed record of the motions of the earth. Thus, a complete elementary seismograph consists of a pendulum, a recording device, and a clock. To get a complete record of ground motion we actually need three seismographs, one to record vertical and two to record horizontal components of motion.

Sensitive seismographs greatly magnify—anywhere from 100 to over 100,000 times—the small tremors of a tiny or distant earthquake. Special strong-motion seismographs are triggered only by strong ground motion,

Figure 11-1 Elements of a simple seismograph for the recording of vertical ground motion. The block, suspension bar, and drum all are attached to the earth and move with it. The suspended mass, held by a spring, remains essentially fixed while the earth moves under it. The drum is rotated by clockwork, and so the pen, or stylus, traces a record of the vertical component of motion on the graph paper placed around the drum.

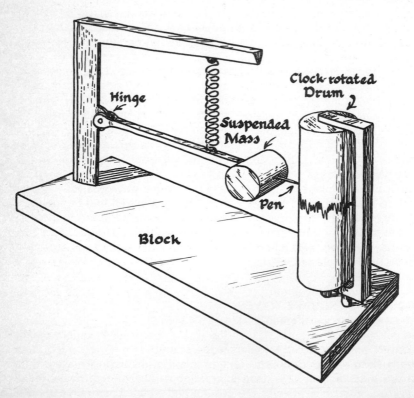

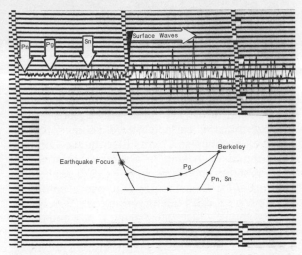

Figure 11-2   The record (seismogram) of a typical California earthquake. At 01:42:19.5 GCT (1 hour, 42 minutes, and 19.5 seconds after midnight Greenwich Civil Time) an earthquake took place off the northern California coast at latitude 40.1°N and longitude 124.4°W, close to the northern end of the San Andreas fault zone. Depth of focus was about 10 kilometers (6 miles), and Richter magnitude computed from the seismogram at the Berkeley Seismographic Station was between 5.8 and 6.0 (BRK 5.8-6.0). The record was made by a Wood-Anderson seismograph which responded to the east-west component of the ground motion. Distance between vertical broken lines on the seismogram represents 1 minute of time. For example, it was about 1 minute after the earthquake occurred that the surface waves began to appear on the seismogram. The seismologist has labeled the first appearance of four kinds of waves: Pn and Pg—fast-moving push-pull waves; Sn—slower waves of distortion; and surface waves. The small inset shows diagrammatically the paths of the P and S waves from the earthquake focus through the crust and mantle to Berkeley. The earthquake was felt as far away as Klamath Falls, Oregon. Chimneys were cracked and people were frightened in the nearby small towns of Petrolia and Honeydew. Several aftershocks occurred. (*Seismogram courtesy of Bruce A. Bolt, Director, University of California Seismographic Station, Berkeley. Reproduced from Gordon B. Oakeshott,* California's Changing Landscapes, *by permission of McGraw-Hill Book Company.*)

either near a moderate earthquake or some distance from a major earthquake. Records of the strong-motion instruments are usually expressed in terms of the horizontal and vertical components of the force of gravity, g. The *direction* of horizontal ground movement may be given in terms such as east-west or north-south.

THE HAZARDS OF EARTHQUAKE WAVES
In Chapter 2, we considered some aspects of earthquake risk and attempted to put earthquakes into perspective in relation to the great disasters of

history. Among the ground effects accompanying and following moderate-to-great earthquakes, what are the most damaging?

Of course, one cannot build any structure on an active fault trace—a fault having caused an earthquake within historic times—without high risk. Equally hazardous is a building on an active landslide; most of the damage done by the 1964 Anchorage, Alaska, earthquake was the result of landslides triggered by the earthquake. However, the largest losses of life and property in earthquake country like California have been caused by violent ground shaking. In other words, the earthquake surface waves account for the greatest losses. According to the Los Angeles County Earthquake Commission (1971), losses due to earthquake shaking in California total $1,156 million. The California Division of Mines and Geology, in its 1973 publication *Urban geology—Master plan for California*, estimates that losses, within the state, due to earthquake shaking will total $21 billion by the year 2000, unless measures are taken to reduce the threat which the shaking of old and poorly constructed buildings poses to life and property.

In order to design and build earthquake-resistant structures, architects and engineers need to learn much more about the motions of structures when Love and Rayleigh waves pass through an area.

SUMMARY

In Chapter 11, we are really talking about the earthquake itself, for, by definition, an earthquake is an abrupt or sudden motion of the earth. So we must investigate the nature of this motion by studying earthquake waves.

There are three principal types of waves: The P wave, which is the "push-pull" type, with particles of earth materials moving parallel to the direction of general movement of the wave; the S wave, which is the shear or transverse type in which the particles vibrate at right angles to those in the P wave; and the surface waves, which are a mixture of several types and which make up most of the earthquake motion as we feel it. P waves are fastest, surface waves are slowest, and S waves move at about two-thirds the velocity of P waves.

Which of these wave types is most destructive to buildings?

Look in an elementary physics book for the section on waves and their behavior; this might help you to get an understanding of earthquake waves.

Records of earthquake waves are made by seismographs. *You* can be a "seismograph" because your body "records" its motion relative to the earth in an earthquake which is strong enough and local enough to be felt. But you are not a very good seismograph because you are not perfectly free to remain motionless while the earth vibrates, and your feelings are so involved that you cannot make an objective record.

Most of the *effects* of earthquake waves we have considered in Chapters 2 and 14.

Why and how can a seismogram show the approximate distance of an earthquake from the seismographic station? How are epicenters located? How could the depth of focus of an earthquake be determined?

Why do you think that California has shallow-focus earthquakes while the Philippines and the Tonga Islands have deep-focus earthquakes?

Why are earthquakes that originate on the San Andreas Fault very shallow-focus (less than 15 kilometers)? This is really a tough question, but worth consideration.

TWELVE

GREAT AND DESTRUCTIVE EARTHQUAKES
IN WORLD HISTORY

ONE OF HISTORY'S GREATEST—LISBON, 1755

How large can an earthquake get? California has had three (1857, 1872, and 1906) in historic times, each with a magnitude of about 8.3. The Alaskan earthquake of 1964 had a magnitude of 8.5. Many earthquakes in modern times have exceeded magnitude 8, but, judging from the felt area and surface effects, seismologists have determined that the great Lisbon earthquake of November 1, 1755, was about 8.9! The strength of the rocks of the earth's crust may well limit earthquake magnitude; the crust would probably rupture by faulting before sufficient stress and strain could accumulate to cause an earthquake of over magnitude 9. Lisbon is located on the north bank of an estuary at the mouth of the Tagus River, about 6 or 8 kilometers inland from the Atlantic Ocean. The epicenter of the earthquake may have been on an east-west fracture zone a few kilometers southwest of the city.

I have an old *Principles of Geology* (1872 edition) by Sir Charles Lyell which gives this account:

> In no part of the volcanic region of southern Europe, has so tremendous an earthquake occurred in modern times as that which began on November 1, 1755 at Lisbon. The inhabitants had had no warning of the coming danger, when a sound like that of thunder was heard underground, and immediately afterwards a violent shock threw down the greater part of their city. In the course of about 6 minutes, 60,000 persons perished. The sea first retired and laid the bar dry; it then rolled in, rising 50 feet or more above its ordinary level.

A new wharf, built of marble, and loaded with people who had fled from the first shock in the city, was overwhelmed by the seismic sea wave, sank, and neither people nor wharf were ever seen again.

Harry Fielding Reid (1914) called it "probably the most notable earthquake in history." He tried to sort out fact from fancy in numerous "historical" accounts. Probably the earthquake was felt as far as Cairo, Scandinavia, the British Isles, and the Canary Islands. Reid thinks that it was felt over an area of 16 million square kilometers or about 6 million square miles. Compare this with a felt area of about 375,000 square miles for Fort Tejon, California, 1857; and 640,000 square miles for Owens Valley, California, in 1872.

The large area over which the Lisbon earthquake was felt, the seismic waves it caused, the numerous seiches (sloshing waves) (Chapter 2) in distant lakes, and the large loss of life all combined to make it "notable." This was the first time in history that seiches in lakes had been correlated with a distant earthquake. At Loch Lomond in Scotland, for example, the water rose as much as 2 feet 4 inches. This was also the first time that serious, scientific explanations were offered for the origin of seismic sea waves or tsunamis.

MISSISSIPPI VALLEY, 1811 AND 1812

Among the most intriguing earthquakes ever felt in North America was the series of three in the Mississippi Valley centering near New Madrid, Missouri, in 1811 and 1812. "Unusual" (all earthquakes are unusual) in many respects, these earthquakes serve as an excellent example of the infrequent, large earthquakes of the Mississippi Valley and eastern North America, in contrast to the frequent earthquakes of California and the West.

Strong earthquakes, centered near New Madrid, occurred on December 16, 1811, January 23, 1812, and February 7, 1812, with magnitudes estimated, respectively, at 7.2, 7.1, and 7.4. Total felt area was about 2.5 million square kilometers. Professor Otto W. Nuttli of St. Louis University, who made a special study of these earthquakes, estimates the total release of energy was equivalent to a magnitude 8.0 earthquake.

Geologically, the area is at the upper end of the great Mississippi River delta and so is a region of thick alluvium. Layers of water-saturated sand liquefied extensively during the earthquakes, resulting in large surface displacements, sand boils, fissures, and landslides. Land subsidence, uplift or doming, and caving of river banks took place over large areas; Reelfoot Lake was formed in Tennessee. There was no single, well-defined surface fault, but a linear region of 140 kilometers (87 miles) long by a few kilometers wide of "major subsidence, doming, fissures, sinks, and large sandblows" was developed.

Most large earthquakes consist of a single major shock followed by a series of much lesser aftershocks; but here were three major earthquakes, rather widely spaced in time. A second anomalous feature was the great area of damage, a felt area about 100 times as great as in an earthquake of similar magnitude in the West.

However, seismologists are finding that in Mississippi Valley and eastern earthquakes the surface-wave energy seems to diminish outward much more gradually than for earthquakes in the West.

How, then, do we estimate further earthquake hazards in the United States east of the Rocky Mountains? Professor Nuttli says:

> The absence of large-magnitude earthquakes in eastern North America since the Charleston, South Carolina earthquake in 1886 has resulted in complacency, or perhaps unawareness on the part of the general populace of the existence of any earthquake threat to them. When such earthquakes of the size of the 1811-1812 sequence occur, the emotional problems which will result for large numbers of people in the widely affected area will likely be severe, particularly if the earthquake energy is released over a long period of time, in the manner of the 1811 and 1812 earthquakes.

HEBGEN LAKE, MONTANA, 1959

For our example of a Rocky Mountain earthquake, we choose that at Hebgen Lake, Montana, of August 17, 1959. This magnitude 7.1 earthquake centered on the north side of Hebgen Lake (formed by an old earth-fill dam across the Madison River) in the Madison Range. The main shock, which came at 11:37 P.M., Mountain Standard Time, originated at depth of not over 25 kilometers and was felt over 600,000 square miles. Twenty-eight people were killed. Although this was a major earthquake—not a great one—I have never seen such a variety of spectacular ground effects in the limited area of about 300 square miles!

My wife, young son, and I had driven from Duluth, Minnesota, a few days after the earthquake, had stopped at Billings to borrow a Montana state geologic map from a friend, and were headed south on U.S. Highway 191 toward Yellowstone. About 8 miles north of West Yellowstone, we came to a vertical drop in the highway about 8 feet high, down-dropped on the south. An overturned car on the down-dropped side suggested that an earlier driver had not seen or heeded the posted warnings.

We shortly discovered that the scarp at Highway 191 was part of the arcuate, northwest-trending Red Canyon fault. Following it to the northwest, we found that it was a normal (tensional) fault with a near-vertical dip, down-dropped to the south, and part of a fault zone in the southern Madison Range which had been reactivated during the earthquake (Figure 12-1). At Blarneystone Ranch, a mile or so northwest of the highway, the scarp was about 14 feet high in alluvium, with a graben at its base. A few miles farther, at Red Canyon Creek, we stood at the base of an extraordinary vertical scarp 20 feet high! On the companion Hebgen Lake fault a similar scarp at Cabin Creek Campground was 15 feet high. All these extremely high fault scarps were in loose alluvium and slide material in the canyons along the mountain front; scarps were much lower where they crossed bedrock. Resurveys have shown that it was largely the down-dropped blocks that moved; the mountain block retained its elevation.

At the Rock Creek Campground—about 6 miles downstream from Cabin

Figure 12-1   Red Canyon fault scarp, Hebgen Lake, Montana, earthquake of August 1959. The man stands on the top of the uplifted block; the base of the vertical scarp is seen in the lower left corner of the drawing, 20 feet below him. The new waterfall was formed in a fraction of a second as fault displacement took place. (How long do you suppose this fall will last? The scarp is in loose rockslide and alluvial material.) (*Peter H. Oakeshott drawing from a kodachrome.*)

Creek—the earthquake triggered an enormous rock slide. Here 43 million cubic yards of Precambrian rock slid down the steep south slope across the Campground and the Madison River and about 500 feet up the north wall. According to those who escaped, a high-velocity wind swept the canyon just ahead of the rock slide. Of the 28 campers killed by the earthquake, 26 were buried here; the other 2 were killed by isolated falling rocks. With the Madison River backed up behind the new rock dam, a lake several miles long—immediately named "Quake Lake"—quickly formed.

Before we left the Hebgen Lake area, it was clear that the lake's northeast margin had subsided several feet, as we could see from drowned shoreline features. Equally clear was the exposed, uplifted southwest margin of the lake. Thus, the lake bed had been tilted.

Later resurveys proved maximum subsidence of the Hebgen Lake basin to be 22 feet. About 50 square miles subsided over 10 feet, and 200 square miles subsided over 1 foot. Subsidence was differential, warping the lake bed and creating a huge seiche that overtopped Hebgen Dam and sloshed water back and forth for about 11 hours.

What was the geologic setting in which the faulting, the warped basins, the subsidence, and the rockslides took place?

The general trend of geologic structures, the mountains, and the Madison River Valley is northwest in this area. The ancient Precambrian and Paleozoic sedimentary rocks were complexly folded and thrust-faulted during great mountain building in the Late Cretaceous and Early Tertiary periods when the Rocky Mountains were built. Then, in latest Tertiary and into Quaternary time, normal faulting took over to form block-fault ranges and basins. The August 1959 faulting was a continuation of this action.

Contrary to any other earthquake we have studied, the people who lost their lives were killed by rockfalls, not by the collapse of buildings. Nowadays, with the congregation of numbers of people in campgrounds in the mountains, the most remote areas become open to geologic hazards!

SUMMARY

Every account of a particular earthquake or a particular volcano which we have given in this book was included because it had lessons, and interest (hopefully!), for us. No two earthquakes are alike and from each one we learn something new.

What did you learn about earthquakes that was completely new to you from Lisbon, Mississippi Valley, and Hebgen Lake? These were chosen partly because they were major or great earthquakes occurring at very different times and places.

Why do you suppose Mississippi Valley, 1811 and 1812, was three separate earthquakes instead of one giant? This is a difficult question to which even seismologists would like an answer! What are the problems of estimating seismic hazards in the United States east of the Rocky Mountains?

The Hebgen Lake earthquake was fascinating because of the very high vertical fault scarps, the tilting of Hebgen Lake (was it really the lake that tilted?), and the huge rock slide that buried so many campers.

We can do much to prepare for and lessen the hazards of earthquakes in metropolitan areas, but what could have been done in the Hebgen Lake area prior to the earthquake to lessen the hazard? Don't give up; there are some things that, reasonably, could have been done.

THIRTEEN

EARTHQUAKE COUNTRY: TWO "MODERATE"
CALIFORNIA EARTHQUAKES

Just as the savanna of East Africa is "elephant country" and the Midwest of the United States is "tornado country," so California is "earthquake country"! Sunset has published (Iacopi, 1964) a charming book on California faults and earthquakes titled *Earthquake Country*.

The fact that California is indeed earthquake country is abundantly clear from its 200-year record since Gaspar de Portolá reported a strong earthquake near the Santa Ana River in Orange County in 1769. Of the thousands of felt earthquakes during these two centuries, at least three—Fort Tejon 1857, Owens Valley 1872, and San Francisco 1906—were truly *great* earthquakes (Richter magnitude greater than 7.7); at least 12—like Arvin-Tehachapi 1952, and El Centro 1940—were *major* earthquakes (magnitude 7.0 to 7.7); and over 60—such as Santa Barbara 1925, Long Beach 1933, and San Fernando 1971 were *moderate* shocks (magnitude 6.0 to 6.9). In addition, about 200 earthquakes per decade in the magnitude range of 4.0 to 5.9 have been strongly felt locally. Some of these smaller earthquakes have produced no real damage; others (Santa Rosa 1969, for example) have produced significant damage.

Since moderate earthquakes are many times more frequent than major and great earthquakes, let us look rather closely at a couple of moderate California shocks whose history, geology, and seismology are well known. Through these two earthquakes we can see what did happen and the kinds of things that might be expected in future earthquakes. This is reason enough for selecting the Long Beach–Compton 1933 and San Fernando 1971 earthquakes, but an added reason is that I was personally, unforgettably involved in each!

LONG BEACH–COMPTON, 1933

It was about 5 minutes to 6:00 P.M. on March 10, 1933, and twilight was beginning to dim the landscape on this rather dull day as seen from our home on the border of Compton and north Long Beach. My wife and I had just returned home after shopping in downtown Compton—at that time a town of about 13,000 people, with its business district concentrated in a few blocks along Main Street.

As we were preparing dinner, I stood at the kitchen window facing south toward what was to be the earthquake epicenter, about 20 miles away. I looked up sharply when I heard a peculiar, low-pitched rumbling sound. Then, within 2 or 3 seconds, came the sounds of crashing buildings, explosions of dust into the air, and violent shaking of our one-story frame-and-stucco house. So fast did the violence follow the first tremors that we barely had time to plant ourselves desperately in the kitchen doorway. My mother and my two-year-old son were thrown to the living room floor and our small, squat, open gas heater was upended.

Checking the sound effects with seismologists through the years has convinced me that we heard the P wave, the fastest of the earthquake waves, which may well have a frequency within the audible range. We failed to identify the slower-moving S waves, but there was no doubt whatever of the quickly following surface (Rayleigh and Love) waves, for our modest house was twisted and rocked by such intense ground motion that we marvelled that our later inspection revealed no real damage.

Seismologists and geologists now recognize that local ground movement in a moderate earthquake—like the 6.3 Richter magnitude Long Beach earthquake—may be as large as in a truly great earthquake, like the magnitude 8.3 San Francisco earthquake of April 18, 1906.

Water, electricity, gas, and phones were all turned off within minutes of the main shock, but not before I had completed a phone call to Oakland to tell our folks that we were safe, and not before we had drawn tubs of water because we feared that the water might be shut off. Services were restored in Long Beach and Compton within a few hours; gas service took longest while emergency utility crews checked systems for leaks.

Judging from the strength and duration of shaking, ground cracking, and concentration of building damage, the intensity of the earthquake was higher in Compton than it was in Long Beach, although Long Beach was closer to the epicenter (Figure 13-1). There appear to be good geologic reasons for this: Compton lies at sea level in a water-saturated basin of loose sediments formed by overflow of the Los Angeles River and Compton Creek, while Long Beach is mostly built on more solid rock, which is relatively more stable in an earthquake.

How long did we feel the intense shaking? A long, long 10 seconds, or more—during which I wondered: to what climax of intensity could this build up? Would the house utterly collapse around us? I experienced the same

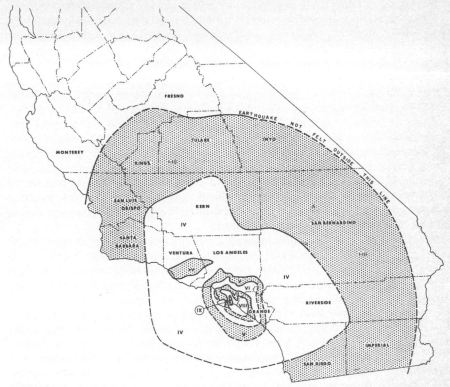

Figure 13-1 Isoseismal map for the Long Beach, 1933, earthquake. The Roman numerals show the range of intensities (Modified Mercalli scale) reported within each zone. *Iso* means equal; so, ideally, an isoseismal map shows zones of equal earthquake intensity. (*California Division of Mines and Geology.*)

uptight apprehension in the strongly felt aftershock of October 2, 1933 (Richter magnitude 5.4), which originated along the same fault northwest of the March 10 earthquake.

In my wisdom (?) as a young geologist, I told my wife that we had certainly experienced the main shock and all aftershocks would be smaller. Therefore, there was no sense in following the neighbors who were moving out onto their front lawns for the night's rest. So, we stayed inside and heard all night long the screaming sirens of the ambulances taking the injured along nearby Long Beach Boulevard into Los Angeles emergency hospitals, and experienced one bed-shaking aftershock after another. Before morning, my 7-months-pregnant wife was shaking in resonance. Needless to say, we moved out on the lawn for the next several nights!

Building Failures   Our house fared well—as did most of the other modern single-story wood-frame houses—but others were not so fortunate. Many of the older, larger wood-frame houses—often set on "cripples," or pedestals, instead of continuous concrete foundations, and not bolted to their foundations—were displaced horizontally 1 or 2 feet and collapsed. Many of the old business buildings, built of unreinforced brick, with poor mortar, and designed only for vertical load and not resistant to the horizontal forces of an earthquake, failed. Even a moderate earthquake imposes stresses and strains on structures which expose weaknesses in design and construction that years of static load might not uncover! I shall never forget one of the "classic" building failures in Compton. My good friend, Dr. Firkins, a dentist who had gone on geologic field trips with me (through the diversion tunnels in the gorge of the Colorado River before the Hoover Dam was built, for example) was killed by a falling beam as he was working on a patient. His office was on the second floor, supported only by vertical "stilts" above an open market. His patient was hurt slightly, but survived. This was a personal tragedy which left a profound impression on us. My wife and I attended outdoor services for him a few days later, held in the backyard of the mortuary as the aftershocks continued.

The worst of all building failures were those which affected the schools of Long Beach and Compton. I shall cite the buildings of the Compton Union High School and Junior College, both because they were typical of "schoolhouse" failures and because in 1933 I was teaching surveying and the earth sciences at the college and so have poignant memories.

Our three-story high school and college classroom-and-administration building was so badly damaged that it had to be razed and rebuilt. My basement classroom was filled with rubble and a central chimney structure had come down through classrooms on two floors into the basement. I managed to salvage surveying equipment in a few days, after the aftershocks died down. It was indeed a godsend that the earthquake happened at a time of day when school buildings were nearly unoccupied. Compton College's beautiful, tile-roofed arcades between buildings collapsed completely. The great and lasting good that came from the tragic and scandalous failures of school structures in this earthquake was the passage of the Field Act by the State Legislature. The Field Act requires state approval and inspection of school buildings, plans, and construction practices. I say "scandalous" failures because the strong shaking of the earthquake revealed shortcuts in construction practices, as well as design, in many school buildings. Experience in later earthquakes—notably Arvin-Tehachapi 1952, San Francisco 1957, and San Fernando 1971—has amply demonstrated the importance of the Field Act in increasing seismic safety of school buildings.

Ground Failures　The swampy, estuarine lowlands in portions of the earthquake area were sites of ground and road cracking, separation of bridge structures from their approaches, and evidence of shallow soil-liquefaction as shown by sand boils and mud volcanoes. Fracturing and dislocation of streets and curbs in the water-saturated, lowland sediments of the Compton basin were extensive. For example, the carefully laid out bench marks I had set on curbs around the college for the use of my surveying students were rendered useless by the extensive breaking and dislocation of the concrete curbs.

Settling cracks in the lowlands and earth slumps and slides along the steeper slopes of the surrounding hills gave testimony of strong ground shaking.

In addition to the direct effects of ground shaking, the many ground breaks and irregular settlement contributed significantly to building and street damage.

COMPTON'S BUSINESS DISTRICT   How could business be carried on? What about essential goods and services for the public?

On the edge of the city—only a few blocks from the old business center—stood the unoccupied huge, boxlike steel-and-galvanized-iron structure of the Fry Roofing Company. A day or two after the earthquake the plan was conceived to lay out "streets" in this vast structure and to allocate to each businessman prorated space in the same relative position and with the same street names to which we were all accustomed. Thus, we all had a big, convenient market for months after the earthquake, while downtown Compton was being rebuilt!

The earthquake had occurred during the worst part of the Great Depression; people had little money and cash was scarce. Before "Downtown Compton" in its temporary setting could be abandoned, a bank moratorium was enforced and all funds were frozen! School employees— teachers and noncertificated—were fortunate to have their contracts paid in full, but for a few months our salary checks were held back, subject to receipt of tax funds by the County.

But the depression and the bank moratorium are only incidental to our earthquake story. They but added to our problems; and—like the earthquake—there were lasting, good outcomes. Out of the earthquake came better construction practices and the Field Act; so, out of the depression and the bank failures came many social and economic reforms, including federal deposit insurance.

After the initial disaster of the earthquake, public enthusiasm for rebuilding became high, and—like the phoenix of old—Compton and Long Beach rose from their "ashes." Homes and public structures were rebuilt—bigger, better, and earthquake-resistant—and the schools were reconstructed, with guarantees of renewed earthquake safety under the Field Act.

Origin of the Earthquake—Newport-Inglewood Fault Zone Ever since modern man began to explore the Los Angeles basin—only about 200 years ago—he has noted a northwesterly trending belt of low, domelike hills which extend for about 40 miles from the Newport area in coastal Orange County to the Cheviot Hills a few miles away north of Culver City in Los Angeles County. By 1920, petroleum geologists had recognized that these hills are the surface expression of a series of structural domes and disconnected faults, and in 1921 petroleum was discovered in the anticlinal dome of Signal Hill—one of the world's great oil fields.

Detailed mapping and study by geologists have since shown that the Newport-Inglewood fault zone is a complex series of faults and folds, geologically active from mid-Tertiary time (40 million years ago) to the present, which may be the shallow expression of a deep-seated fault zone. It was along one or more of the faults near the southeastern end of this Newport-Inglewood zone that abrupt displacement took place to cause the Long Beach–Compton earthquake and aftershocks.

Although no surface fault breaks were found in 1933, analysis of the seismograms of the earthquake suggests that the displacement was such that the western block was moved northward relative to the eastern block, as along the San Andreas Fault, with the focus offshore at a depth of about 10 kilometers.

Significantly, deep drilling has shown that the Newport-Inglewood fault zone probably separates the complex late Jurassic (?) "Catalina Schist" on the west from Cretaceous (?) granitic bedrock on the east which underlies the main Los Angeles basin.

SAN FERNANDO EARTHQUAKE, 1971

Just before daylight at 6:01 on February 9, 1971, the San Fernando region was shattered by one of the most devastating earthquakes in California's 200-year earthquake history. Sixty-four lives were lost, many more were injured, and property damage was over $500 million. It was the third worst in California history in terms of lives lost (San Francisco 1906 and Long Beach 1933 were greater), and was exceeded only by San Francisco in terms of property damage.

Although only a moderate earthquake—magnitude 6.5—its occurrence on the northwestern margin of Los Angeles in the San Fernando Valley directly affected a population of over a million people.

This time I was not there to feel it, but the earthquake held an especial interest for me because I had mapped this very area and worked out the patterns of faulting and sequences of rock formation in the early 1930s. So it was "my" earthquake!

Geologic Setting   The big picture of what happened, geologically, is now clear. A block of the high, rugged San Gabriel Mountains (one of the Transverse Ranges), including a surface area of at least a hundred square miles, moved upward about 2 meters relative to San Fernando Valley on its south and shifted westward as much as 2 meters. This reverse oblique slip took place along a highly irregular, curved fault surface dipping about 55° northward at the focus, which was about 8 kilometers deep in the heart of the old crystalline rocks of the western San Gabriel Mountains (Figure 13-2). Seismological data show that movement on the fault surface progressed upward and southward (toward the San Fernando Valley) at a rate of about 2 kilometers per second. As the fault approached the surface its dip lessened until it was less than 20° where the fault met the surface. Thus, this earthquake originated in displacement along a reverse or thrust fault—like Arvin-Tehachapi in 1952—in contrast to all other known California earthquakes, which have resulted from movement on strike-slip or normal faults.

How does this behavior fit into what we know of the geology of the area? What has been the late history of faulting, folding, and mountain building in this region?

Figure 13-2 Looking east along the trace of the San Fernando Fault across the mouth of Lopez Canyon, San Fernando earthquake of February 1971. The surface fault can be followed as a sinuous line along the base of the hills from lower left to upper right in the photo. The San Gabriel Mountains were elevated as much as 2 meters and thrust out over the San Fernando Valley. (*Courtesy of California Division of Mines and Geology.*)

Rock formations in the San Gabriel Mountains include most major rock types in great variety, ranging from Precambrian igneous and metamorphic rocks to young river deposits. The Precambrian crystalline rocks consist principally of anorthosite and related types, radiometrically dated as being 1.2 billion years old, which have intruded the 1.4 billion-year-old Mendenhall Gneiss. Mesozoic granitic rocks, at least some of which have been dated at about 70 million years old, have intruded the older rocks.

The crystalline rocks which form the central core in the highland part of the San Gabriel Range are flanked on the north, west, and south by overlying younger Tertiary and Quaternary sedimentary and volcanic rock formations which are 70 million to less than 1 million years old.

The structure of the San Gabriel Mountains is very complex, but most pertinent to our present consideration is the fault zone along the mountain front called the Sierra Madre fault zone. This comprises a series of discontinuous reverse faults which extends for about 12 miles along the south front of the western San Gabriel Mountains and the northern margin of the San

Figure 13-3 Damage typical of that which occurred to the new freeway bridge structures, San Fernando earthquake of February 1971. (*Courtesy of California Division of Mines and Geology.*)

Fernando Valley. These are arcuate, convex-southward, reverse faults which generally separate the crystalline rocks on the north from the Tertiary and Quaternary sedimentary formations on the south. The faults are discontinuous, with dips ranging from 15° to vertical; all dip northward, with the crystalline rocks thrust upward toward the south over younger sediments.

The youngest of the faults in the Sierra Madre fault zone is the San Fernando Fault, which caused the earthquake. Thus, essentially the same pattern of faulting and mountain-building uplift appears to be continuing today as has marked the mountain building of the last million years!

Surface Faulting, Ground Breaking, and Landslides Complex ground breaks mark the trace of the San Fernando Fault for over 12 miles in an east-to-west direction. A series of discontinuous, curved fault scarps— uplifted on the north side—from a few centimeters to about 1 meter high was formed. Height of the south-facing scarps averaged about $\frac{1}{2}$ meter. They are asymmetrical, compressional features which some of the field geologists described as being "like a wave breaking upon a beach." Across soil and grassy fields the fault traces resembled a giant mole track. Clumps and pieces of sod were often overridden, overturned, or crumbled. Multiple scarps were common.

Besides the traces of the causative San Fernando Fault, abundant ground cracks emphasized the areas of most intense shaking. Some of the tops of ridges seemed to have literally exploded, with the ridge crests resembling plowed fields where the soil has been overturned. Such shattered ridge crests are attributed to very high vertical ground acceleration. At Pacoima Dam, on gneissic bedrock about 8 kilometers south of the earthquake epicenter, a maximum ground acceleration of 1.25 g was recorded. The largest acceleration ever recorded before that was 0.5 g!

Over 1,000 landslides in a 250 square kilometer (100 square mile) area of the mountains were triggered by the earthquake and its aftershocks. These included all types, from soil flows, formed by liquefaction of sediments on valley-floor slopes of less than 1°, to rockfalls in the steep mountains.

Structural Damage   Most often, death and injury in earthquakes are caused by the failure of man-made structures. Of the 64 deaths at San Fernando 44 happened when old unreinforced masonry buildings collapsed at the Sylmar Veterans Hospital. More sobering, however, was the loss of 3 lives in the new reinforced concrete buildings of Olive View Hospital.

Modern one-story frame houses partly collapsed in many instances but generally caused no loss of life. Schools built since the 1933 Field Act performed well in the earthquake; older schools fared not so well. New high-rise buildings in nearby downtown Los Angeles suffered no structural damage.

By far the most spectacular structural damage was the complete collapse of a number of new, very high, reinforced concrete freeway bridge structures (Figure 13-3). But more serious was the disruption of countless utility lines—gas, water, sewer, power, and telephone. It took weeks to fully restore these services.

The most frightening event was the near-failure of an old hydraulic earth-fill dam (Figure 13-4) which was severely damaged and almost released the water behind it down across a residential area of 80,000 people!

SUMMARY

Moderate earthquakes—in the magnitude 6 range—in many ways merit more study than major and great earthquakes, mainly because there are so many more moderate earthquakes. So our planning for the mitigation of earthquake hazards should, in large measure, be directed toward the more frequent moderate earthquakes. We have chosen two from California because they caused a great deal of damage to common types of building structures, their histories are well known, and both scientists and the public learned a great deal from them. For example, California's damages to school buildings were drastically cut by legislation—including the Field Act— (Chapter 14) after the Long Beach, 1933, earthquake.

No geological event is more personal—and more terrifying—than a strong earthquake. Even in a volcanic eruption, one usually has time to get to a place of personal safety and to watch matters with a more-or-less detached viewpoint. There is no such thing as a "detached viewpoint," however, for the person caught in an earthquake. So, I have written about these two earth-

Figure 13-4 Lower Van Norman Dam after the 1971 San Fernando earthquake. Settling, partial liquefaction, and sliding in the earth fill of this old dam endangered 80,000 people living below it. (*Los Angeles Times photo, courtesy of California Division of Mines and Geology.*)

quakes from a very personal viewpoint with the hope that something extra might be learned from my experience, plus the basic scientific facts that are available. Which of the personal remarks told you something that you didn't know about earthquakes?

In what respects was the San Fernando earthquake different from the Long Beach–Compton earthquake? In what respects were they alike?

After the San Fernando earthquake, seismologists and geologists recognized that local intensity and ground motion near the epicenter of a moderate earthquake can be as great as in a great earthquake. How then, does a great earthquake differ in its action and effects from a moderate earthquake?

What geological and historical conditions known prior to the Long Beach earthquake could have raised warning signals concerning the possibility of an earthquake?

What might have been done prior to the San Fernando earthquake to reduce possible structural damage and loss of life?

FOURTEEN

PEOPLE, PROTECTION, AND PREDICTION

No more spectacular natural processes affect people on this earth than the geologic violence of volcanoes and earthquakes. In Chapter 2, we considered a history of some of the great disasters of all time and the part that earthquakes and volcanoes have played in this history. Earthquake risk is real—in earthquake country like California, Alaska, and Japan! No less real is the volcanic hazard of Hawaii, Iceland, or Sicily!

Our approach in this little book has been a scientific—geologic— consideration of volcanism and earthquake activity, but not without implications of their effects on people.

Let us now reflect a little more specifically on "people effects"— socioeconomic aspects, if you like.

EARTHQUAKE PROTECTION: A CONTINUING PUBLIC PROBLEM

The California Division of Mines and Geology, in its *Urban Geology—Master Plan for California* (Alfors et al., 1973), estimates that losses to the state of California due to earthquake shaking will total $21 billion from 1970 to 2000, and that losses from volcanic activity may total $50 million in the same period, *unless more protective measures are taken*. The National Oceanic and Atmospheric Administration estimates that there could be as many as 10,000 deaths and 40,000 hospitalized injuries from an 8.3 magnitude earthquake on the San Andreas Fault near San Francisco. Many earthquake scientists believe that this is an extreme viewpoint.

Of course, California is "earthquake country," but no part of the world is free from earthquakes. Recall, for example, the great Lisbon earthquake of 1755 and the Mississippi Valley earthquakes of 1811 and 1812, both of which occurred in areas where earthquakes are infrequent.

How can the earthquake challenge be met? We should learn all we can about earthquakes—their occurrence, their causes, and what happens during an earthquake. Then, we can plan for tomorrow's earthquakes.

What Can Government Do?   The action of government is principally along two lines: legislation and administration, planned for loss reduction. Fortunately, most earthquake damage to property and most loss of life are preventable.

California's Division of Mines and Geology urban master plan says:

Recommendations for reducing losses from geologic problems fall into two major categories: (1) those that propose to improve the state of the art by developing new capabilities, and (2) those that propose to extend the application of present state-of-the-art procedures. In general, a sequence of steps is required for any effective action program to reduce losses due to geologic problems. First, the nature and severity of the problem must be recognized. Second, solutions for the problem need to be devised where possible. Third, contingency plans and preparations need to be made for responding to those problems that cannot be solved adequately. Fourth, long-range recovery actions should be planned for the catastrophic problems (like earthquakes and volcanic eruptions).

If current practices were upgraded to the current state of the art and all presently feasible loss-reduction measures were applied throughout California, an estimated $38 billion reduction in losses (for all kinds of geologic hazards in [this earthquake state]) could be realized by the turn of the century. The total cost of applying the loss-reduction measures is estimated to be $6 billion, and the overall benefit to cost ratio over 6 to 1.

In order to effect greater loss reduction, remedies other than those currently known and being applied would have to be devised and used. For example, breakthroughs in earthquake prediction and earthquake control could result in large reductions of projected losses due to earthquake shaking.

Losses in earthquakes could be substantially cut by enforcement of improved building codes to ensure better earthquake-resistant design. Most loss of life in earthquakes (but not all; see Hebgen Lake earthquake, Chapter 12) is due to collapse or partial collapse of buildings. Really hazardous, poorly designed and poorly built structures should be demolished. Maybe something can be done on this by offering reduced taxes to owners who abolish unsafe buildings.

Land-use zoning can be every effective in reducing losses, with geological examinations and recommendations of all lands being subdivided for residential and commercial use. The addition of geologists to planning and engineering staffs of local government can go a long way toward preventing hazardous locations of structures.

In California, significant measures to reduce earthquake hazards have been developed by the Legislature's Joint Committee on Seismic Safety and by the Governor's Earthquake Council, and much has already been accomplished through administrative action which has redirected program priorities of state agencies.

What Can We Do in Our Homes? The California Division of Mines and Geology has some good advice for our actions, *before*, *during*, and *after* an earthquake:

Before:

1. Potential earthquake hazards in the home should be removed or corrected. Top heavy objects and furniture, such as bookcases and storage cabinets, should be fastened to the wall and the largest and heaviest objects placed on lower shelves.

2. Supplies of food and water, a flashlight, a first aid kit, and a battery-powered radio should be set aside for use in emergencies.

3. One or more members of the family should have a knowledge of first aid procedures because medical facilities nearly always are overloaded during an emergency or disaster, or may themselves be damaged beyond use.

4. All responsible family members should know what to do to avoid injury and panic. They should know how to turn off the electricity, water, and gas; and they should know the locations of the main switch and valves.

During:
The most important thing to do during an earthquake is to remain calm. If you can do so, you are less likely to be injured. Motion during an earthquake is not constant; commonly, there are a few seconds between tremors.

1. If you are inside a building, stand in a strong doorway or get under a desk, table, or bed. Watch for falling plaster, bricks, light fixtures, and other objects.

2. Do not rush outside. Stairways and exits may be broken or may become jammed with people. Power for elevators and escalators may have failed. If you are in a crowded place such as a theater, athletic stadium, or store, do not rush for an exit because many others will do the same thing.

3. If you are outside when an earthquake strikes, try to stay away from high buildings, walls, power poles, lamp posts, or other structures that may fall. If you are in an automobile, stop in the safest possible place, which, of course, would be an open area, and remain in the car.

After:

1. After an earthquake, the most important thing to do is to check for injuries in your family and in the neighborhood. Seriously injured persons should not be moved unless they are in immediate danger of further injury. First aid should be administered, but only by someone who is qualified.

2. Check for fires and fire hazards. If damage has been severe, water lines to hydrants, telephone lines, and fire alarm systems may have been broken; contacting the fire department may be difficult. Some cities, such as San Francisco, have auxiliary water systems and large cisterns in addition to the regular system that supplies water to fire hydrants. Swimming pools, creeks, lakes, and fish ponds are possible emergency sources of water for fire fighting.

3. Utility lines to your house—gas, water, and electricity—and appliances should be checked for damage. If there are gas leaks, shut off the main valve which is usually at the gas meter. Do not use matches, lighters, or open-flame appliances until you are sure there are no gas leaks. Do not use electrical switches or appliances if there are gas leaks, because they give off sparks which could ignite the gas.

4. Water lines may be damaged to such an extent that the water may be off. Emergency drinking water can be obtained from water heaters, toilet tanks, canned fruits and vegetables, and melted ice cubes. Toilets should not be flushed until both the incoming water lines and outgoing sewer lines have been checked to see if they are open.

5. There may be much shattered glass and other debris in the area, so it is advisable to wear shoes or boots and a hard hat if you own one. Broken glass may get into foods and drinks. Liquids can be either strained through a clean cloth such as a handkerchief or decanted. Particular checks should be made of the roof line and in the attic because unnoticed damage can lead to a fire. Closets and other storage areas should be checked for objects that have been dislodged or have fallen, but the doors should be opened carefully because of objects that may have fallen against them.

6. Do not use the telephone unless there is a genuine emergency. Emergencies, damage reports, alerts, and other information can be obtained by turning on your radio. Do not go sightseeing; keep the streets open for the passage of emergency vehicles and equipment.

7. Stay away from beaches and other waterfront areas where seismic sea waves (tsunamis or "tidal waves") could strike. Also stay away from steep landslide-prone areas if possible, because aftershocks may trigger a landslide or avalanche, especially if there has been a lot of rain and the ground is very wet. Also stay away from earthquake-damaged structures.

8. Parents should stay with young children who may suffer psychological trauma if parents are absent during the occurrence of aftershocks.

9. Cooperate with all public safety and relief organizations. Do not go into damaged areas unless authorized; you are subject to arrest if you get in the way of, or otherwise hinder, rescue operations. (*Your area is likely to be under direct military authority.*)

10. Send information about the earthquake to the United States Geological Survey, Golden, CO. First, secure the proper reporting form from the Survey.

BENEFITS FROM VOLCANOES
Are there any things good, or beneficial, about volcanic eruptions and great earthquakes? Yes, many! The beauty of majestic volcanoes is certainly a benefit (Figure 14-1). The very existence of places like the Hawaiian Islands, Yellowstone, Iceland, the island arcs of the world—like the Aleutians—and

Figure 14-1   Mt. St. Helens, elevation 9,671, one of the most beautifully symmetrical of the Cascade volcanoes, northeast of Portland. It last erupted in 1854, and, like Mt. Hood, could endanger Portland by floods and mudflows when it erupts again. (*Austin Post photo, U.S. Geological Survey.*)

the volcanoes of the Mediterranean, where thousands can view these natural wonders, is a marvelous benefit.

Volcanic eruptions and earthquakes are examples of geologic violence, but they are not necessarily geologic disasters or geologic hazards. There is nothing basically "good" or "bad" in natural geologic events; there are no geologic hazards, or disasters, without people. And there is much that intelligent people can do to avoid disaster, or ease it when it threatens.

Much newly erupted volcanic rock is highly porous, both the lava in flows, and the volcanic fragments which may range from dust-sized particles to large blocks. The surfaces of lava flows are rough and uneven and the rock is full of *vesicles*—holes left by escaping gases—as well as cracks, fissures, and other openings, all of which collect wind-blown dust, water, and organic matter. In a warm, moist climate like that of Hawaii such rocks weather very fast and are soon covered by tropical vegetation. I visited Kapoho, a few miles south of Hilo, Hawaii, in 1966 and found fractures and uneven surfaces on the 1960 lava flows already supporting a new growth of lichens and ferns.

Lava flows and volcanic ash make fertile soils and new eruptions form topsoils rich in mineral elements; the necessary organic matter is soon added. Winds spread volcanic ash over thousands of square miles, adding to the fertility of soils throughout the world. Particularly in the tropics, where soils are subject to very rapid leaching, the renewal of fertility by new layers of volcanic materials is vital. Central America, the Philippines, and Java are such areas. In soils in the middle latitudes of the western United States (for example, the Sonoma Volcanics in the wine country north of San Francisco) and in the Mediterranean region, volcanic materials are of major importance. Mount Vesuvius in Italy has had a history of intermittent explosive activity spanning over 2,000 years, with periods of quiescence sometimes lasting several hundreds of years. Because of the fertility of Vesuvius' volcanic soils, farmers have cultivated their vineyards and crops even up into the very crater itself during the periods of inactivity of this great volcano.

Volcanic rock itself is widely useful in many applications. In many parts of the world, volcanic rock may be the only type available. (Where, for example?) It is crushed and used for road base all over the world, it has been quarried and cut into building blocks; the more exotic and highly colored rock is valuable for ornamental purposes, and "garden" rock is a large business. Some of the glassy, porous types of volcanic rock—like *pumice* and artifically expanded *perlite*—make strong, lightweight aggregate for building. Some of the huge blocks of *obsidian* from Glass Mountain in northern California have even been polished for mirrors! Volcanic ash which has weathered to a clay called *bentonite* is a much-used product in the petroleum industry in well drilling. Name a need for rock and somewhere you'll find volcanic rock in use!

PREDICTION OF VOLCANISM—MONITORING THE GREAT VOLCANOES
The prediction of volcanic eruptions, in general, is reasonably valid, but to specify precise time of an eruption of a volcano is another matter. (See Figure 14-2.)

Figure 14-2 Mt. Hood, towering 11,245 feet above sea level east of Portland, Oregon. It is a typical composite volcano of the Cascade Range which, like the other cascade volcanoes, should not be considered extinct. Hood erupted sometime around 1801. An eruption of Mt. Hood could endanger the city of Portland by pouring vast quantities of mud and water into tributaries and reservoirs upstream from the Columbia River. (*Austin Post photo, U.S. Geological Survey.*)

Monitoring of active volcanoes has reached a high stage of development at the Hawaiian Volcano Observatory on Kilauea. A slight ground swelling precedes eruptions as hot magma rises toward the surface. The swelling is noted by measuring increases in the lengths of horizontal lines, local increases in elevation, and by measuring surface tilt by tiltmeters on the slopes of the volcano. Seismographs at Kilauea, and at other active volcanoes, commonly record a great increase in the number and magnitudes of minor earthquakes preceding an eruption, sometimes beginning months ahead of an eruption but increasing in strength and frequency until eruption occurs. Most of the earthquakes which occur before and during volcanic eruptions are due to subsurface movements of magma and to the explosive activity, but occasionally larger and deeper earthquakes suggest breaks on rifts or fault zones. During 1973 the Hawaiian Islands had a magnitude 6 earthquake which did some damage at Hilo. Naturally, ground temperatures increase also as the magma rises before an eruption.

The U.S. Geological Survey is now monitoring more volcanoes around the world by installing seismographs and tiltmeters, and by observing hot spots and changes in the activity of fumaroles. Worldwide surveillance of volcanoes is being appreciably aided by observations from the Earth Resources Technology Satellites of the National Aeronautics and Space Administration. Eventually, we shall have a volcanic-eruption warning system, something like the seismic sea-wave warning system of the National Ocean Survey.

BENEFITS FROM FAULTS AND EARTHQUAKES

It might be difficult to conceive of an earthquake as an asset, but certainly earthquake-causing faults make great contributions to our environment.

Faults play a major part in mountain building and in a great variety of our principal landforms. Examples are many. The eastern side of California's Sierra Nevada presents one of the highest and most magnificent mountain slopes in the world; glaciated, saw-toothed ridges, capped by Mount Whitney at elevation 14,496 feet, tower above the 4,000-foot floor of Owens Valley. The great escarpment is basically the result of a series of uplifts along the complex Sierra Nevada fault zone; the latest was an abrupt upward displacement, leaving a *scarp* (step) as high as 23 feet at the base of the mountains, in the Owens Valley earthquake of 1872. All over the world we find our highest, geologically youthful mountain ranges flanked and molded by faults. Volcanoes make mountain *peaks* but faults make mountain *ranges*!

Faults have been major contributors to some of our most magnificent landforms, from mountain ranges to lakes and stream valleys. They have also entered into the formation of many of our economic mineral deposits, have effected the location of harbors, and have modified our climates. Faults may act as channels to carry mineral-bearing solutions and thus may localize ore bodies; they may also displace and offset ore bodies which have already been formed. Faults often act as channels for water, and also as barriers to the passage of water through the openings in rock underground.

Surely, the benefit-to-cost ratio of faults is overwhelmingly favorable!

Deepening Knowledge of the Earth's Interior Volcanic eruptions and great uplift by faulting both bring us samples from below the earth's surface, far out of reach of the deepest mines or even of the deepest wells drilled for oil. Still, the deepest-seated rocks that reach the surface for us to study come only from the base of the earth's crust and the upper mantle.

How, then, do we know that the earth is made up of layers of rock materials of different densities, that there is a solid metallic core at a depth of about 5,155 kilometers surrounded by a liquid outer core, and that there are other layers in a complexly stratified earth (Figure 14-3)?

Almost all our information comes from studies of earthquake waves—their characteristics, their velocities, and how they are refracted and reflected

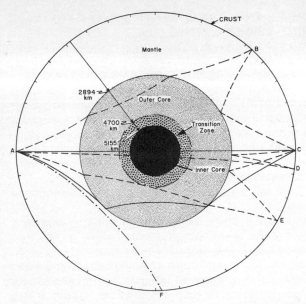

Figure 14-3 Interior of the earth, as inferred from the recorded passage of earthquake waves. Assume an earthquake takes place at *A*. Then about 90° away around the earth the earthquake is recorded directly at seismograph station *F*; this P wave has moved through the mantle only. A slightly steeper wave from *A* that happens to be just tangent to the outer core is refracted to station *C* at a distance of 180° around the earth. Other lines show other ray paths as they have actually been recorded in earthquakes. (*Diagram from Bruce A. Bolt, Professor of Seismology, University of California, Berkeley. Reproduced from Gordon B. Oakeshott,* California's Changing Landscapes, *by permission of McGraw-Hill Book Company.*)

as they encounter rock materials of different properties and densities. Some seismologists—like Dr. Bruce A. Bolt, head of the Seismographic Station, at the University of California at Berkeley—have undertaken such studies as lifetime research projects.

Finding Oil and Other Minerals If earthquakes can tell us so much of the interior of the earth, why not use them to get subsurface information on the properties and structures of rock formations, faults, folds, and boundaries of strata, which might aid in exploration for ore bodies, petroleum, and natural gas?

This has, indeed, been done. Seismologists have set up artificial earthquakes by exploding charges in shallow holes in the ground, and by dropping heavy weights. Precisely timed nuclear blasts, with known energy inputs, have also been applied to gain information below the earth's surface. Large areas where bedrock is concealed by thick alluvium—such as the Gulf Coast of the United States and the Great Central Valley of California—have been very successfully explored for rock structures favorable for the occurrence of petroleum and natural gas since growth of the use of artificial earthquakes began in the early 1930s.

PREDICTION OF EARTHQUAKES—SCIENTIFIC DREAMS OR REALITY?

In 1958, Dr. Charles F. Richter, professor of seismology at the California Institute of Technology, wrote of the "will-o'-the-wisp" of earthquake prediction. Dr. Perry Byerly, Professor Emeritus, University of California, answers questions about the next earthquake by advising, "The longer it's been since the last, the sooner the next one will come." Other seismologists have proposed intensive research programs aimed at the goal of earthquake prediction, a goal some consider attainable within a few years.

First of all, what are we talking about when we consider earthquake "prediction"?

Obviously, prediction involves place, time, and magnitude; or where, when, and how big? The historic and geologic records show *where*, in a general way, for earthquakes repeat themselves. Fault movements recur on the same old breaks, or related faults, and certain geologically young areas have a relatively high seismicity. But, every so often an earthquake occurs where it was not expected—Charleston, 1886, for example. Within a very active seismic area there may be many active faults, but which one of these will rupture next? As yet, we have no specific answers to these problems, but we do know, for example, that the next earthquake in California is more likely to originate on the San Andreas Fault than in the center of the Sacramento Valley.

When will the next earthquake occur? Again, we can easily speak in generalities, but we have few specifics. We cannot say that an earthquake will occur next week in a given locality, but we can say that a major damaging earthquake originating on the San Andreas Fault is likely within the present century. Until we know much more than we do now, Dr. Byerly's answer is about as well as we can do.

As far as magnitude is concerned, we can again predict *generally*. Earthquakes can be expected to recur along faults with the same maximum magnitudes as they have had in the past. We know, also, that the greater the length of an active fault, the greater the earthquake may be. But *segments* of long faults rupture to cause small earthquakes, also. Review Chapter 10 on the earthquake history of California's San Andreas Fault, which gives us concrete evidence on these very points.

How big? Histories of fault and earthquake activity are our best guides.

Clues to Earthquake Prediction   Basically, if we could measure the rate of accumulation of strain along an active fault, and if we knew how much strain the rocks could stand before breaking, we could predict time, place, and magnitude of a fault break and the resulting earthquake.

Precise surveying measurements along and across faults are helping. Instruments called *tiltmeters*—and natural tiltmeters like the surfaces of water bodies—have sometimes recorded tilt of a land surface prior to an earthquake. Laser beams are being used to make very precise measurements of distances. Of course, some earthquakes are marked by foreshocks. One of the problems is: How do we recognize a foreshock as such? Swarms of very small earthquakes (less than magnitude 2) measured by seismographs along active fault zones may be preliminary to larger shocks, but are not always so.

A very promising new concept referred to as *dilatancy* is currently (1974) being investigated. Russian seismologists found that the ratio of the velocities of compressional (P) waves to shear (S) waves consistently dropped below its average value and then increased to the average value before small-to-moderate earthquakes. Artificial earthquakes may be used to obtain data on wave velocities which can be useful in dilatancy studies. "Dilatancy" refers to increase in volume, or swelling, of rock material as many tiny fractures open in the rock prior to an earthquake. Dilatancy may be recognized by changes in ground elevations, lengths of surveyed lines, changes in electrical conductivity, and emission of the radioactive gas, radon. Research to date is inconclusive and conflicting.

Consequences of Earthquake Prediction   What if we *could* accurately predict earthquakes in time, place, and magnitude? What sorts of social and economic problems would we then face?

Imagine broadcasting a prediction that San Francisco would suffer a great earthquake tomorrow! Think of the insurmountable problems of evacuation of the people in this city of 700,000 whose Golden Gate Bridge to the north, Bay Bridge to the east, and Bayshore Freeway to the south are jammed with traffic even at normal commuting times. What would people do to save their worldly goods as well as take care of their personal safety and that of their families?

We have a long way to go before we can handle the "weather forecast" type of earthquake prediction!

A LOOK AT THE FUTURE—EARTHQUAKE CONTROL?
Having pursued the "will-o'-the-wisp" of earthquake prediction at least briefly, and having left unanswered our headline question "Scientific dreams or reality?", we take another step into the future to look at the possibilities of *earthquake control.*

Amazingly, this is no farther out than earthquake prediction. From 1962 to 1965, Denver, Colorado, had over 700 small earthquakes, ranging from 0.7 to 4.3 magnitude. This was an unprecedented increase in seismic activity, for history shows this to be a region of low seismicity (infrequent small earthquakes).

What had happened? Consulting geologist D. M. Evans found that there was a direct relationship between the injection of waste water into a 12,045-foot disposal well at the Rocky Mountain Arsenal and the earthquakes.

After intensive experimentation, the U.S. Geological Survey concluded that the Denver minor earthquakes had indeed been caused by the building up of fluid pressure in fractures and faults in rock at depth. Since that time, controlled experimentation by the U.S. Geological Survey at the Rangely,

Colorado, oil field has shown that the injection of water builds up pressure and causes fault slippage and earthquakes; withdrawal of fluid reduces pressure and brings a reduction in the incidence of small earthquakes. Would this work in other areas, like a portion of the San Andreas Fault which is locked and under great accumulation of strain? If so (and we think it would), how about reducing the strain before it accumulates to the breaking point by deliberately causing some small earthquakes to relieve the strain?

But who would dare to inject water into the great San Andreas Fault? How would we know just how much and not too much? Is it possible that we would trigger a great and damaging earthquake?

Perhaps our present policy should be one of cautious restraint, experimentation, and intensified efforts to maximize the learning from earthquakes.

SUPPLEMENTAL READING

In writing this little book on volcanoes and earthquakes I have assumed that the reader has at hand the minimum library resources of the student: Dictionary and Atlas. No words or terms that cannot be found in Webster's Collegiate Dictionary have been used.

Following is a list of readily available, low-cost books and papers, which I think will be helpful to you if you are looking for more about earthquakes and volcanoes.

Alfors, John T., Burnett, John L., and Gay, Thomas E., Jr., 1973, Urban geology master plan for California, *California Division of Mines and Geology*, Bulletin 198, 112 pp. (The nature, magnitude, and costs of geologic hazards in California and recommendations for their mitigation.)

Algermissen, S. T., 1969, Seismic risk studies in the United States, Proceedings of the Fourth World Conference on Earthquake Engineering. (Technical explanation of the basis for construction of the Seismic Risk Map of the United States.)

American Geological Institute, 1973, *Investigating the earth*, 529 pp. (See Harris et al.)

Association of Engineering Geologists, 1973, *Geology, seismicity, and environmental impact*, Special Publication, University Publishers, Los Angeles, Calif., 445 pp.

Bailey, Edgar H., (Ed.), 1966, *Geology of northern California*, California Division of Mines and Geology. (A group of many papers and field guides covering much of the geology of California north of the Tehachapi Mountains. Contains much on volcanism, faults, and earthquakes.)

Barazangi, Muawia, and Dorman, James, 1969, World seismicity maps compiled from ESSA, Coast and Geodetic Survey, epicentral data, 1961–1967, *Seismological Society of America Bulletin*, vol. 59, no. 1, pp. 369–380. (First of the world seismicity maps which make use of the modern, superior, seismograph coverage and data processing techniques.)

Barrows, Allan G., 1973, Earthquakes along the Newport-Inglewood structural zone, *California Geology*, March, 1973, California Division of Mines and Geology, pp. 60–68. (Geology and earthquake history related to the 1933 Long Beach earthquake. See also Oakeshott, in the same issue, pp. 55–59.)

Bolt, B. A., Horn, L., MacDonald, G. A., and Scott, R. F., *Geological hazards*, Springer Verlag New York Inc., New York, 1975.

California Division of Mines and Geology, 1971, *California Geology*, April–May, pp. 59–84. (Special San Fernando earthquake edition, containing a series of articles by geologists of the State Division of Mines and Geology on all facets of the earthquake.)

California Division of Mines and Geology, 1971, Earthquakes—Be prepared!, *California Geology*, Nov. 1971. Reprinted as *Special Publication 39*, April 1973. (A brief but wide coverage of occurrence of earthquakes, causes, prediction, list of California earthquakes, seismic risk maps, and what can be done before, during, and after an earthquake.)

California Division of Mines and Geology, 1972, The great Owens Valley earthquake of 1872, *California Geology*, March, pp, 51–64. (A complete account of one of California's three greatest earthquakes.)

California Geology (successor to *Mineral Information Service*), a monthly journal which includes many issues dealing with earthquakes and volcanoes, California Division of Mines and Geology, Room 1341, Resources Bldg., Sacramento, Calif., 95814.

California Legislature, 1971, *Earthquake risk conference proceedings*, September 22–24, 1971, Joint Committee on Seismic Safety, 777 N. First St., Suite 600, San Jose, Calif., 95112. (A collection of short papers by recognized authorities on most aspects of earthquake risk.)

California Legislature, 1974, *Report of the Joint Committee on Seismic Safety*, Joint Committee on Seismic Safety, 777 N. First St., Suite 600, San Jose, Calif., 95112. (A comprehensive series of 4-year studies on engineering, earthquake sciences, governmental organizations and performance, land-use planning, disaster preparedness, and postearthquake recovery.)

California, State of, 1972, *First report of the Governor's Earthquake Council*, Governor's Office, State of California, Sacramento, 65 pp. *Second Report*, September 1974, 86 pp.

Coffman, Jerry L., and Cloud, William K., *United States earthquakes, 1968*, National Earthquake Information Center, Rockville, Md., 20852, $1.50.

(Includes map of the U.S. showing damaging earthquakes, 1769–1968.)
Crandell, D. R., and Mullineaux, D. R., 1967, Volcanic hazards at Mount Rainier, Washington, *U.S. Geological Survey*, Bulletin 1238. (Study of the characteristics and geologic history of a great composite volcano.)
Crandell, Dwight R., and Waldron, Howard H., 1969, Volcanic hazards in the Cascade Range, *Geologic hazards and public problems*, Office of Emergency Preparedness, pp. 5–18.
Field, Harry Fielding, 1914, The Lisbon earthquake of November 1, 1755, *Seismological Society of America Bulletin*, vol. 4, no. 2, pp. 53–80.
Giggenbach, Werner F., Kyle, Philip R., and Lyon, Graeme L., 1973, Present volcanic activity on Mount Erebus, Ross Island, Antarctica, Geological Society of America, *Geology*, vol. 1, no. 3, November, pp. 135–136.
Green, Jack, and Short, Nicholas M. (Eds.), 1971, Volcanic land forms and surface features: A photographic atlas and glossary, Springer-Verlag New York Inc., New York, 519 pp. (198 beautiful plates, with short explanatory texts.)
Grove, Noel, 1973, A village fights for its life, *National Geographic Magazine*, vol. 144, no. 1, July, pp. 40–67. (A colorful account of the world's latest significant volcanic eruption, Iceland.)
Harris, Miles F., Hesser, Dale T., Hynek, J. Allen, Matthews, William H., III, Roy, Chalmer J., Skehan, James W., S. J., and Stevenson, Robert E., 1973, *Investigating the earth*, Houghton Mifflin Company, Boston, 529 pp. (A modern earth-science textbook based on the original Earth Science Curriculum Project of the American Geological Institute. Good reading from junior high shcool to college levels; well illustrated.)
Hill, Mary R., 1965, Earth hazards, California Division of Mines and Geology, *Mineral Information Service*, vol. 18, no. 4, pp. 57–59. (An editorial, with a summary of some of the world's great disasters.)
Hodgson, John H., 1964, *Earthquakes and earth structure*, Prentice-Hall, Inc., Englewood Cliffs, N.J. (Good reading for beginning students.)
Hunt, Charles B., 1972, *Geology of soils—Their evolution, classification, and uses*, W. H. Freeman and Company, San Francisco. (Geologic aspects of formation, development, and uses of soils, including those of volcanic origin.)
Iacopi, Robert, 1964, *Earthquake country*, A Sunset book, Lane Book Company, Menlo Park, Calif., 192 pp. (How, why, and where earthquakes strike in California. Well-illustrated, popular account of California's earthquakes and their causes. Foreword by the noted seismologist, Dr. Charles F. Richter.)
Leet, Lewis Don, and Leet, Florence, 1964, *Earthquake: Discoveries in seismology*, Dell Publishing Company, Inc., New York. (Elementary discussion of causes and mechanism of earthquakes.)
Lyell, Sir Charles, 1872, *Principles of geology*, 11th ed., vol. II, pp. 147–154. (Lisbon earthquake of 1755.)
Macdonald, Gordon A., 1972, *Volcanoes*, Prentice-Hall, Inc., Englewood Cliffs, N.J., 510 pp. (Modern, comprehensive coverage of all forms of volcanism and volcanoes.)
Macdonald, Gordon A., and Abbott, Agatin T., 1971, Volcanoes in the sea:

The geology of Hawaii, University of Hawaii Press, Honolulu. 441 pp. (Comprehensive, up-to-date treatment of the geologic processes that have formed the Hawaiian Islands.)

Matthews, Samuel W., 1973, This changing earth, *National Geographic Magazine*, vol. 143, no. 1, January, pp. 1–37. (Excellent popular account of sea-floor spreading and continental drift, and their relationships to volcanoes and earthquakes; spectacular illustrations.)

Matthews, William H., III, 1969, *The story of volcanoes and earthquakes*, Harvey House, Inc., Irvington-on-Hudson, New York, 126 pp. (A well-written, well-illustrated, popular account.)

McNitt, James R., 1963, Exploration and development of geothermal power in California, *California Division of Mines and Geology Special Report 75*, 45 pp. (More recent information available from California Division of Oil and Gas, Resources Bldg., Sacramento, Calif., 95814.)

National Oceanic and Atmospheric Administration, 1971, Seismic risk map for conterminous United States, *Earthquake Information Bulletin*, March–April and May–June 1971. (Divides the U.S. into 4 zones ranging from no reasonable expectancy of earthquake damages to maximum damage which may occur.)

National Oceanic and Atmospheric Administration, 1972, *A study of earthquake losses in the San Francisco Bay Area*. (Data and analysis.)

National Oceanic and Atmospheric Administration, 1973, *A study of earthquake losses in the Los Angeles, California, area*, 329 pp. (Analysis of damages that might be expected from great and major postulated earthquakes; historical earthquakes.)

National Oceanic and Atmospheric Administration, Leonard M. Murphy, Scientific Coordinator, 1973 (Released in 1975), *San Fernando, California, earthquake of February 9, 1971*. (A set of three volumes: vol. I, *Effects on building structures*; vol. II, *Utilities, transportation, and sociological aspects*; vol. III, *Geological and geophysical studies*.)

Nuttli, Otto W., 1973, The Mississippi Valley earthquakes of 1811 and 1812: Intensities, ground motion, and magnitudes, *Seismological Society of America Bulletin*, vol. 63, no. 1, pp. 227–248. (Most complete account and modern analysis of this great series of earthquakes.)

Oakeshott, Gordon B. (Ed.), 1955, Earthquakes in Kern County, California, during 1952, *California Division of Mines*, Bulletin 171, 283 pp. (A symposium of the stratigraphy, structural geology, and origin of the earthquakes; their geologic effects; seismologic measurements, application of seismology to petroleum exploration; structural damage and design of earthquake-resistant structures.)

Oakeshott, Gordon B., 1958, *Geology and mineral deposits of San Fernando quadrangle, Los Angeles County, California*, California Division of Mines, 147 pp. (Includes geologic, structural, and fault maps of the area of the 1971 San Fernando earthquake.)

Oakeshott, Gordon B., 1964, The Alaskan earthquake, California Division of Mines and Geology, *Mineral Information Service*, July, pp. 119–121, 124–125. (Summary account of principal geologic factors and damage.)

Oakeshott, Gordon B., 1971, *California's changing landscapes*, McGraw-Hill

Book Company, New York, 388 pp. (A guide to the geology of the state; includes geologic principles of broad application; many illustrations. Comprises geologic principles and processes, a chronological account of geologic formations and history, and guides to the geologic features which can be seen from California's major highways. Self-explanatory for high school and college students and amateur geologists.)

Oakeshott, Gordon B., 1973, 40 years ago—The Long Beach–Compton earthquake of March 10, 1933, *California Geology*, March, California Division of Mines and Geology, pp. 55–59. (Eyewitness account. See also, Barrows, in the same issue, pp. 61–68.)

Oakeshott, Gordon B. (Ed.), 1975, San Fernando earthquake of 9 February, 1971, *California Division of Mines and Geology*, Bulletin 196, 463 pp. (Compilation of many papers on the geology, seismology, and structural damage.)

Office of Science and Technology, 1970, *Task Force on Earthquake Hazard Reduction*, Executive Office of the President, September 1970, Superintendent of Documents, Washington, D.C., 20402, 55¢. (A series of recommendations to develop a national action program for reduction of loss of life and property damage in earthquakes.)

Richter, Charles F., 1958, *Elementary Seismology*, W. H. Freeman and Company, San Francisco, 768 pp.

Scientific American, 1970, *Continents adrift*, W. H. Freeman and Company, San Francisco. (Original readings from the world's leading authorities; many diagrams, maps, and photos.)

Seismological Society of America Bulletin, 1911 to present. (Technical accounts of most of the world's earthquakes; developments and research in seismology; engineering seismology.)

Stearns, Harold T., 1966, *Geology of the State of Hawaii*, Pacific Books, Publishers, Palo Alto, Calif., 266 pp. (Detailed coverage of each island; should be studied with the author's *Road guide*.)

Stearns, Harold T., 1966, *Road guide to points of geologic interest in the Hawaiian Islands*, Pacific Books, Publishers, Palo Alto, Calif., 66 pp. (Self-guided geological tour of the principal islands; glossary.)

Steinbrugge, Karl V., 1968, *Earthquake hazard in the San Francisco Bay area: A continuing problem in public policy*, Institute of Governmental Studies, University of California, Berkeley. (Discussion of public policy problems in an area of high population and earthquake frequency, by a well-known structural engineer.)

Steinbrugge, Karl V., and Cloud, William K., 1962, Epicentral intensities and damage in the Hebgen Lake, Montana, earthquake of August 17, 1959, *Seismological Society of America Bulletin*, vol. 52, no. 2, pp. 181–234.

Tarling, Don, and Tarling, Maurine, 1971, *Continental drift: A study of the earth's moving surface*, Doubleday and Company, Inc., Garden City, New York, 140 pp., $1.95. (Short account in a small paperback, by two people who accept the concepts of plate tectonics more as fact than hypothesis or theory.)

Thorarinsson, Sigurdur, 1967, *Surtsey: The new island in the North Atlantic*, The Viking Press, New York.

Tocher, Don, 1962, The Hebgen Lake, Montana, earthquake of August 17, 1959, MST, *Seismological Society of America Bulletin*, vol. 52, no. 2, pp. 153–162.

United States Geological Survey, 1966, *The Alaska earthquake, March 27, 1964: Field investigations and reconstruction effort*, U.S.G.S. Professional Paper 541, 111 pp. (A good, profusely illustrated introduction to the story of a great earthquake—its geologic setting and effects, the field investigations, and the public and private reconstruction efforts.)

United States Geological Survey, 1972, *Atlas of volcanic phenomena*, U.S.G.S., Washington, D.C., 20242, $4.25 per set of 20. (A beautiful series of highly colored plates, or posters, each about 15 × 19 inches, accompanied by brief, explanatory texts. Excellent photos and diagrams. All the principal features of volcanoes and volcanism are represented.)

United States Geological Survey, Washington, D.C., many free, short pamphlets on geological subjects with titles such as *Volcanoes, Geysers, Earthquakes*, and *Natural steam for power*.

U.S. Office of Emergency Preparedness, 1969, *Geologic hazards and public problems*, May 27–28, 1969, Conference Proceedings, Office of Emergency Preparedness, Region Seven, Federal Regional Center, Santa Rosa, Calif., 95403. (Twenty authoritive papers on a wide variety of earth hazards—including earthquakes and volcanoes—and programs for their mitigation.)

Verhoogen, John, Turner, Francis J., Weiss, Lionel E., Wahrhaftig, Clyde, and Fyfe, William S., 1970, *The earth, an introduction to physical geology*, Holt, Rinehart, and Winston, Inc., New York, 748 pp. (A comprehensive summary of basic knowledge of physical geology. Thorough coverage of igneous phenomena, of volcanism, and of earthquake mechanism.)

Williams, Howel, 1941, *Crater Lake: The story of its origin*, University of California Press, Berkeley.

Williams, Richard S., Jr., and Moore, James G., 1973, Iceland chills a lava flow, *GeoTimes*, August, pp. 14–17. (Account of a remarkable experiment to control lava flows on the island of Heimaey.)

Wilson, J. Tuzo, 1963, Continental drift, *Scientific American*, April. (Basic, early, scientific paper on seafloor spreading, continental drift, and convection currents in the mantle as the cause.)

Witkind, Irving J., Myers, W. Bradley, Hadley, Jarvis B., Hamilton, Warren, and Fraser, George D., 1962, Geologic features of the earthquake at Hebgen Lake, Montana, August 17, 1959, *Seismological Society of America Bulletin*, vol. 52, no. 2, pp. 163–180.

INDEX

Page numbers in *italic* indicate photographs and figures.